T0341404

Tales Out of School

Poets on Poetry   **Donald Hall, General Editor**

Robert Creeley

Tales Out of
School

SELECTED INTERVIEWS

Ann Arbor

THE UNIVERSITY OF MICHIGAN PRESS

Copyright © by the University of Michigan 1993
All rights reserved
Published in the United States of America by
The University of Michigan Press
Printed and bound by CPI Group (UK) Ltd, Croydon, CR0 4YY

1996   1995   1994   1993   4   3   2   1

Library of Congress Cataloging-in-Publication Data

Creeley, Robert, 1926–
    Tales out of school : selected interviews / Robert Creeley.
        p.   cm. — (Poets on poetry)
    ISBN 978-0-472-09536-0 (sqb)
    ISBN 978-0-472-06536-3 (pbk)
    1. Creeley, Robert, 1926–   —Interviews. 2. Poets,
American—20th century—Interviews. 3. Poetics. I. Title.
II. Series.
PS3505.R43Z475   1994
811'.54—dc20   93-30195
                                                                        CIP

A CIP catalogue record for this book is available from the British Library.

Were our songs of the universe and our visions of that great Love who once appeared to Dante holding his smoking heart in his hand, were our feelings and thoughts that had flowed out of whatever originality they might have had into their origins in phrasings of melody, were our dreams and our architectures to come home at last members of no more than a classroom education?
—Robert Duncan, "Ideas of the Meaning of Form"

Preface

Expectably enough the interviews here collected from a diversity of others are a nearly anthropological evidence, if nothing else, that there was indeed a person as "myself" somewhere consistent with a world now well past but still as inexplicable as when it first all began. The questions and answers comprising the five parts of this book will prove beyond the shadow of a fictive doubt that an "I" was "there," and that "he" made persistently evident all the usual rhetorical apparatus and determination necessary to keep afloat the boatlike "self" one presumes to be the point of one's existence. Or at least this one did at the time.

Robert Graves had written in his introduction to *The White Goddess* (1948), "Poetry is that art for which no academy exists." No place could be more the fact of such judgment than the United States then seemed. There were certainly orthodoxies, dogmatic workshops, hoary institutions, and endless, exhausting opinions, but never the grove or garden belonging to a specific person wherein a Plato, who hardly approved poets to begin with, might confer with peers concerning the apparent nature of this human enterprise and the obvious factors pertaining. Ours was an art otherwise founded, and it has never enjoyed any rule that was not determined by its own intuitive constitution. Ezra Pound's contempt for critics "busily measuring the Venus de Milo" echoes through all the professionalism of my art that I have ever been party to. "By ear, he sd . . ." was Charles Olson's compact assertion of Pound's enduring premise.

When I finally got to England in 1964, I presumed I'd come to the land where poets might expect to enjoy authority, given all those who had provided that "hallowed realm" with such articulate and enduring definition. Yet, as Adrian Mitchell was to tell me, poets came a little after TV reviewers (he was both) in public esteem and use. Nonetheless they had a presumed "history" for solace. No wonder we gave such time to theory, so specifically constructed our verses, and so rehearsed their procedures for any and all who would listen.

No doubt such implicit rawness kept me tight and defensive for years, because I felt I was fact of a poetry that had little apparent definition and certainly no tradition wherewith I could deflect the largely negative judgments one had commonly to deal with. My heroes were often more battered than any pariahs I might imagine: Williams called "anti-poetic," Hart Crane a "failure," Zukofsky "the figment of Pound's imagination," and Pound himself the fascist anti-Semite, rightfully confined in a hospital for the criminally insane. Pound had been passed over by my college teacher as too chaotic and politically abhorrent, while the rest I note were thought too minor to be fit for study. The stakes in that respect were clear from the start and here my apparent defenses are rehearsed repeatedly, going over the premises again and again, the literal ground whereon one had chosen (or been chosen) to make a stand.

I don't think I could responsibly say just what a "poem" was in those days, not in the way one might speak of an apple or Joyce Kilmer's depressing "tree." Even now I'd be wary of the question. I know what I *think* one is, and so will you on reading—but that only begs the question. "Was that a real poem or did you just make it up yourself. . . ." It remains a haunting dilemma.

Yet back of any such question is the very real event of one's life and the world in which one is given to live it. Poetry at the outset of my own particular commitment to its art is an apparent orthodoxy, or at least its powers are so represented. All the variousness possible it seemed had been made static by the overriding authority of the "classical" work of T. S. Eliot and the poets and critics alike for whom he served as defining tradition. The box so created was confining in every way, no matter Eliot's own gifts as a poet. There was simply *le poème bien fait,* or nothing.

So one was again "American" in the crassest of necessities, or else accepted the model which the echoes of a fading English practice still managed to keep dominant. By the mid-sixties, when the first of these interviews took place, the battle was clearly on and even some dissident and neglected British poets had been enlisted. It remains a curious point of fact that Britain's great poet of the period, Basil Bunting, is secured by Pound's initial interest and friendship and by his peers, the American Objectivists, particularly Louis Zukofsky. In 1964, just a year before the Berkeley Poetry Conference, no one in England could tell me where he was to be found, so our unexpected meeting in Newcastle, only a week or so later, was a great surprise and delight. The person who introduced us was the young Northumbrian poet Tom Pickard, whose Morden Tower readings, together with his magazine, *King Ida's Watch Chain,* linked Americans with the contesting and excluded British poets of the time.

Once on the railway platform in Cambridge, England, after having read the night before and now on my way to Norwich for another, I felt nervous and displaced, wondering as ever what it was I thought I was doing and, even more, how I'd come to be in such a place. Thus distracted, I was suddenly brought to my senses by a person's asking me where one should be to get the train to Norwich and at what time was it expected. He turned out to be an Irishman on his way to Norwich also, where, he said, one could find excellent wood for making pipes. He was getting some for a friend and fellow musician because the latter would not come himself to England for all the old reasons. We sat together on the train and he told me of his various travels with his group, and when I told him I had been in Cambridge to read my poems, he reached into his back pocket for his wallet and asked if he might purchase a copy of my book. Characteristically I had no other copy than the one I used for reading, itself a sad instance of the limit of my own powers.

Particular now in mind is the story he told me of the elder

fiddle player who usually went with them on their travels. He said they would be at some festival in southern France, say, where not one of their audience could understand their speech. But still before each song he played, the fiddler would tell how he had come to know it, and who had first played it for him, and what mode or manner he had then learned from some other fiddler's way of playing it. And on and on and on. Yet, for me and my company, this is finally all that matters: how you've come to know what you know, and how you've learned it. It matters to tell it, whether or not it's understood, because it is the clearest way of respecting what has come before and what will follow.

I am much less certain about interviews, but these five were managed with people I both respected and liked. There was always the slight awkwardness of having to deal with the recording, just the mechanicalness of its demand. But these *were* friends, very much so in their generosity to me. Otherwise there is really no rhetorical mode, call it, for the well turned or tuned interview. Or if there is, I have not come upon it nor really ever looked for it at all. God knows any of this could have been continued, like they say. But there was always other work to do, real or imagined.

Buffalo, New York
October 27, 1992

Robert Creeley

Contents

Contents

With John Sinclair and Robin Eichele

The summer of 1965 was a turning point for all of us. The Vancouver Poetry Festival in 1963 had been the intimate and particularizing groundwork, bringing together Charles Olson, Allen Ginsberg, Robert Duncan, Denise Levertov, Gary Snyder, Philip Whalen, Margaret Avison, myself and many others for concentrated yet remarkably comfortable workshops, lectures and readings. It was there that the continuity began to discover itself in poets like Clark Coolidge and Michael Palmer.

Now things got more public, and Ed Dorn, Michael McClure, Diane di Prima, Joanne Kyger, Ed Sanders, John Wieners, Lew Welch, Leonore Kandel all added to the company with, again, many more. So there was much in mind to get said. John Sinclair and Robin Eichele I had met in Detroit, where they with active company had got together the grassroots Artists Workshop, which managed everything from venues for readings to theater, gallery and workshop space around that city. Their formal connection was with Wayne State University, but they were intent on making a place in the city for independent and local artists of all kinds. The interview was for their magazine Whe're 1 *(Summer 1966, p. 2).*

Later Robin started his own film company, doing documentary and recording work of various kinds. John, from Flint, Michigan, who had thought to equip himself to teach school, went through two jail sentences in what was to be one of the most insistent national protests of the criminalizing of marijuana. So, like it or not, he became a political hero of the period. Closer to home, he was a crucial entrepreneur in the jazz, blues and rock scenes and at one point was key figure in the commune, the Rainbow People, next to the university in Ann

Arbor. Our talking here was done during the festival in Berkeley, where Ed Sanders had stuck felt letters spelling "The Fugs" on the back of his t-shirt and none of us knew just how much "the times, they are a-changing . . . . "

Eichele: Bob, I'd like you to introduce things, to give us a brief biographical background.

Creeley: Well, it's simply done. I was born in New England, in Arlington, Massachusetts. My father was a doctor, and I was the younger of two children, my sister being four years older than me. Then he moved us out into the country and he died very shortly after that. My mother, now faced with the problem of bringing us up, went back to nursing which she'd done prior to marrying. She was the public health nurse in the town I really grew up in, a small sort of farm town about 25 miles from Boston, to the north, up past Concord: low hills, orchard country, chicken farmers and some dairy, and a railroad line through the center of the town, a drug store, post office, town square, watering trough—that kind of environment. We stayed there pretty steadily till I was about 13 or 14, and then we heard through my sister of a small school and I managed to get a scholarship. So I spent the high school years in that school in Plymouth, New Hampshire. And then, as my sister married and moved about in her own terms—she married a fellow from Maine and she was very young—I remember we moved as a family to be near her. I don't think it was Mother's intent to intrude on her, but I think she wanted to be close in case there was any kind of difficulty. And then we moved to Cambridge, Massachusetts. I subsequently, after finishing high school, went to Harvard for all but the last of my senior year. I had married in the meantime.

These were very confused years, the war years; I can remember the constant shift and change of the educational form trying to deal with that stretch. They were using an accelerated program trying to rush people through before they became involved with the army. A very chaotic time indeed. I emphasize it because it's the background for Allen Ginsberg, myself and many of our contemporaries. The disturbance of these years came at the end of the Depression and the chaos of values and assumption of values, the definition of values, was very insistent. For example, although we had no knowledge literally of one another, Allen and I had many friends in common at that time. William Cannister was perhaps the most painfully vivid instance of one of "the best minds of [our] generation" that one saw "destroyed by madness." Bill had the compulsive need to kill himself and this need was almost a societal condition, I mean it was almost the actual situation of feeling in those years: a sort of terrifying need to demonstrate the valuelessness of one's own life. Think of the parallel of Existentialism, for example; the whole context of thinking in that time is incredibly self-destructive.

I went into the American Field Service in 1945 and I consequently spent a year in the so-called India-Burma theater, driving an ambulance. So I came back sharing at least that kind of experience with the many persons who were returning then from the war to Harvard to finish that scene. My friends at that time told me a lot about things I really didn't know anything about. For example, music. I just had had violin lessons as a kid. I never learned to play the violin. Anyhow, I was aware that music existed, and so when I got to college—I'd come to college with some sense of Woody Herman, with a general sense of what a *kind* of music might be, but with no specific instance. So there was the possibility of hearing what could be more a deliberated or refined instance of this kind of scene. It was friends in college, for example, who first played me "Billy's Bounce" or "Now Is the Time"— and this was a time when Charlie Parker certainly was *present*. So all that music became known to me and was fascinating to me, if not in an extensive manner, still with very actual intensity. I mean, this is the time of the whole cult of the hipster, the forties designation, the whole thing of being "hip" or "with it"—when a lot of the idiom got located, that is. "Make it," for example, is a very significant expression of that time. Things were "the most," you know, so it was "the most" this and "the most" that. In any case, it was a time when one wanted desperately an intensive and an absolutely full *experience* of whatever it was you were engaged with. So Charlie Parker—think of his place in Jack Kerouac's writing—became kind of a hero of this possibility. I think of the clubs around Boston at that time, where frankly the kids with the background I had, college kids, would really go and sit very goddamned humbly, very very humbly indeed, in the periphery of this activity. Not at all like this sense one finds now, hanging around New Haven, for example: I was taken to a club where the Untouchables were playing and the college boys of that group and that place were all but arrogant and I was a bit dismayed.

Sinclair: It's the same with jazz audiences now—

Creeley: Right—

Sinclair: I know; I grew up with that, must have been a nineteen-forties sensibility and when I first started to hear jazz I would go to a club and sit and hope I might get to meet a musician.

Creeley: Audiences were really very humble at that time, especially if they felt they didn't have means for an immediate response. This is significant: John Chamberlain, the sculptor, whose first wife is a black girl, a singer, and John had the same appetite to get it on; he came from Rochester, Indiana. Everyone was looking for where it was happening and desperately wanted to be accepted by it, because frankly the society as it then was, coming back from the war and realizing home and mother just wasn't, no matter how lovely, any great possibility. And equally the fade-out of the whole sense of being *professional:* trying to become a doctor, a lawyer, the value of one's life as a progression toward some attention was gone because the war demonstrated that no matter how much you tried, as Morganthau said: *facts have their own dynamic*—and this could never be anticipated by any form of adjustment. Anyhow, so those were the years that I began to hear jazz for the first time, of this kind, Charlie Parker and the whole range of those very, to my mind, significant people.

Thelonious Monk, of course, is the kind of man who not

only survived but continued right through this whole period. And, as I say, drummers like Max Roach and those early groups, which one wouldn't want to do without, Al Haig, for example. Jacki Byard was then playing in Boston. Dick Twardzik was another brilliant pianist from Boston; he was with a group when he would have been 14, or something like that, in 1946—like men who couldn't play on union terms but could pick up a gang of teenage kids and have bands, really—I wish I could remember the names of them. I remember the first time I ever saw Dick Twardzik: he was sitting on a piano stool that he could barely reach from, this gangly kid with this dead-set face and utter composure. I mean you could tell from his dress he had nothing else he could offer but his ability to play the piano. He could probably not articulate any other part of his identity, but that piano was really what he knew and so here he would be with this blond-maned character, I wish I could remember his name, a Stan Kenton type, you know, *hope,* played this golden trumpet—

Sinclair: Pomeroy? Was it Herb Pomeroy?

Creeley: Maybe. Anyhow it was someone who really collected this gang of emaciated kids and made, you know, fantastic sounds. Then there were places like the High Hat which is now a garage and gas station, and the Club Savoy, I think it was called.

So there was an interesting flux in jazz. One of my first friends was a young trumpet player, Joe Leach, from around Detroit and he came to Cambridge, to go to college—and he told me an awful lot about jazz without, you know, *telling* me. I think he was doing the same job you have, John, for *Downbeat* for a time. I remember his family were old-time Dixieland people who wanted to keep their kids out of it, you know, and all three children managed to learn to play whatever it was interested them with the family's absolute disagreement. That's sort of random but I want to give some sense of that time. This is what I was doing from 1946 to 1950. I was frankly doing almost nothing else but sitting around listening to records, which my first wife would be pleased to testify to. I listened to records. I was *fascinated* by them; well, first of all, not at all easily, I was fascinated with what these people did with *time*. Not to impose this kind of intellectual term upon it, as I'd question that; but I want to emphasize this was where I was hearing "things said" in terms of rhythmic and sound possibilities—you see, Auden was the alternative if one was depending on reading. But I should make clear Henry Miller was the hero of these years, Kenneth Patchen was the hero of these years, D. H. Lawrence was the hero of these years, Hart Crane—they were the people who kept saying that something *is* possible, it's possible to *say* something, you really have access to your feelings and can really use them as a demonstration of your own reality. You can write directly from that which you feel, and these musicians made clear how *subtle* and how so-phisticated, not simply sophisticated as a kind of social label, but how *refined* that expression might be. I think that's what really attracted me to them; they were *not dumb*. I don't think I could ever be interested in dumbness as a way of life. In fact, how to keep alive was so much involved with how sharp you could be. So these were those times: the same man who played the first Charlie Parker record I ever heard was the same man who gave me the first book of Ezra Pound's that I read.

Sinclair: That's the same experience I had. The guy laid *Howl* on me.

Creeley: I married the last of my time in college; I married, say, the last of my junior year and survived the first of my senior year and then quit. At that time I had friends local to the college scene: the people I really feel significant in that sense, not as influences upon me in an obvious way but friends, as Jack Hawkes, the novelist—he was really a key figure for me at that time—I knew, for example, Kenneth Koch and *liked* him but I had no real intimacy with him of any kind.

There was a group centered around a magazine called *Wake*, which began almost as a demonstration that the *Harvard Advocate* was not to be the only possibility for writing at the college, which was so vast that no one knew what it was, any-how. Thousands of people. So *Wake* was our protest of our exclusion from that possibility. I should also say I later became a very suspect member of the *Harvard Advocate*. At the time it was barely existing, and was subsequently closed down completely by the actions of another musician friend, actually from Cleveland; he began to take drugs, so he began taking books out of the *Advocate* library, which had signed Eliot editions, etc., to sell them, you know. I could only watch in fascination. It seemed to me that they were fairly useless things that he was getting rid of, and I, you know, it was an instance of *property*, I was still worrying about whose books they were and really would continue to but Jack didn't really care about *whose* books they were. So at that time I had these kinds of friends. Then I married and moved to Provincetown, really on the strength of a friendship with the first real writer I was to know, a man named Slater Brown, who was sort of down on his luck at that time, who is happily not at all involved with such problems presently.

He was extremely generous with me; he had been a close friend of both Cummings (he is the character "B" in *The Enormous Room*) and Hart Crane, in fact, one of the few people consistently sympathetic to Crane's situation. Crane had many supporters all through his life but they often became curiously critical of him, people who really liked him for his vitality and intelligence but then began to be all hung up with his conduct. He was not an easy man to be friends with, apparently. In any case, Slater listened to me, not just as my rambling then might have gone on, but he paid me the respect of taking me seriously in my own intentions. He was a very good friend indeed. So we moved to Provincetown and lived there about a year.

I should note, because it's relevant, that I wasn't working during these years; I had no job. We were living on the income that my wife had from her trust fund, a small amount of money that really postponed the actual engagement with how *do* you live in the world. The novel I've written, *The Island*, really gives the content of those years. It isn't the story of my life but it makes much use of that time. In any case, I had all during this time no real sense of being a writer in any way; it was just an imaginative possibility that I really wanted to try to get to. I mean I wanted to write desperately; I wanted that to be it. But at the same time I couldn't demonstrate any competence in it. The connection with Jack Hawkes led me to being published in the issues of *Wake* that he was involved with. But it was a long time before I had an active nucleus of people I worked particularly in relation to—as, for example, Olson or Blackburn, who was my first acquaintance with this kind of person. That chance hearing of Cid Corman's program on the Boston station led to many relationships. By that time we had moved from just outside Provincetown to New Hampshire where we had a kind of rundown farm and I remember we were endlessly trying to repair the house.

We had this plan of having a garden, which we did have, and it gave us potatoes and corn and beans and all that. I was absorbed with pigeons and chickens; I was really fascinated by both of them. I was raising a variety of breeds and I had a very good friend at that time named Ira Grant, who any breeder of Barred Rocks would remember; he was a very, *very*, you know, *great* old man. I learned more about poetry as an actual activity from raising chickens than I did from any professor at the university. I learned more from this chicken farmer about how do you pay attention to things. He had no embarrassment confronting his own attention. He did not try to distract you with something else. It's stupidly placed perhaps in this situation and context, but I one time wrote to a man named Charles Schultz in Lincolnwood, Illinois, about a particular pigeon he had raised that won a national award as a grand champion, a big competitive possibility, and I wrote to him about this particular bird. I'd seen its picture and it was really a lovely pigeon, a lovely thing, and I said how did you breed it, what's the breeding on the bird, and this letter came back with painstaking script, that sort of lovely old man's handwriting, a farmer's handwriting somehow and, you know, *my dear sir, my dear Mr. Creeley*, whatever, with the address and all this business and then followed, "In 19—" (I can't remember the exact year) the letter began like, "In 1908 I secured from so-and-so at such-and-such a place two pairs of such-and-such a pigeon." And he gave the history of that bird, and I thought, God, this is more serious than anything anyone ever said to me in the university. I didn't know this is the patience that's necessary.

That sort of circumstance taught me a lot more than what I was previously involved with. In the meantime obviously I was reading and had happily good occasion to, but I was embarrassed to find out at times how involved I was with poultry, and yet these men curiously allowed me *all* my enthusiasm. I mean, take the Red Pigmy Pouters, which I bred: all the dominant terms in judging this bird for exhibition are based on *recessive* characteristics. I mean almost every feature of this bird, the distinguishing marks which are used in its judging, are almost all without exception recessive: its globe, the way the bird stands, the length of its legs, even the color, the characteristics to which these breeders give attention are almost all recessive—like the *red* color, that's a recessive color for these birds, and it's very interesting that this should have been the color for the grand champion of that year.

Eichele: That was when?

Creeley: The late forties.

Eichele: Took about forty years to put it together—

Creeley: Yeah. This was a young bird, literally a young cock, and this means the bird is one year or younger. There are two classes for age in shows: young bird and old bird; "old bird" is anything over a year old. Well, after the first molt, they molt once, but the characteristics of the color particularly, and the feathering, can change very drastically in that molt so that a young bird of this kind might be useless in another year as a show bird. So they also taught me the fragility of the situation, these people, and they also taught what can matter, you see, so many of us are concerned with the significance of our activities; that is, I think a lot of people have a common embarrassment, one might say, in thinking of poems as an actual thing they might engage their attention with because they say it doesn't count, and what does a poem have to do with the world, I mean it's very interesting to read and feel this man's emotions concerning this or that situation but this doesn't, you know, pay the gas bill—but you see these men with their pigeons cut through all that and, god, they were a lovely range of person: they go all the way from literally multi-multi-millionaires like Edgar Ball, who would give up a cattle show where he was showing his prize cows, would give up the possibility of going there to come to Boston to watch the judging of the Bald Head Tumblers, you know, *or* equally the man who might live in Boston, Massachusetts, and who had just a small coop out back and this was his scene too—so, frankly, there was a lovely democracy you see, because all that really meant anything was the particular bird and that bird *did* have or perhaps not simple parallel but actual parallel with the circumstances in poetry: it was human *attention* given to the possibilities of human life. The bird was as perishable, as fleeting, and as useless as anything can be—I mean, god, the Pigmy Pouter is of no use to anyone in the sense that you don't make any money from it. No one, I'm sure, makes a living from raising pigeons unless they're for the public market in the sense of food.

Sinclair: And how much pigeon can you eat?

Creeley: Not too much—

Eichele: Did the situation occur that sometimes does happen in, say, cattle shows; the grand champion being sold for fantastic amounts of money for a stud?

Creeley: No, because that's another interesting thing about pigeons. A bird that gets to be a champion is a *show bird;* it's a very careful vocabulary. But then you have what are called *stock birds* and stock birds are the birds that are used, frankly, in breeding show birds. Stock birds may have overemphasized characteristics. Then you do get into genetics. But a stock bird is a very distinct bird in that it is used in breeding the qualifications, the qualities you want to have in breeding a bird that will then be used for show. But a show bird is oftentimes of no use as a breeder at all. I mean, he's just a moment in time. I remember one instance of pigeons I was given as a kid—I had an interest early—a pair of fantails, a very common bird around New England. Once you got past icehouse pigeons, the pigeons you could get by climbing up into icehouses or whatever they nest in, and taking the young two or three week old birds out of the nests, getting young *squeakers* as they call them—once you get past that you then went to homing pigeons, *homers* we used to call them, or fantails—these were very common varieties. Well, this one pair of fantails I was given suddenly bred a fantastically good fantail. But I was a kid; I didn't know anything about banding, and you can't show birds without having them banded; that's part of the etiquette in the show scene. This bird was what we call a sport; he was suddenly a lucky strike in the genetic situation. But I mean that taught me to pay attention to a lot of things. I'm surprised now; I haven't been engaged with pigeons for almost fifteen or more years—almost twenty years now—and yet the habits of that attention as we're now talking is so precise that they give me the vocabulary immediately. I mean, I couldn't tell you the same kind of detail about the method of scanning a line of poetry or various systems of metric that are involved with descriptions of poetry. Now I found that one information was useful and felt right in my environment; not that I wanted to be only a pigeon man but I mean that kind of information taught me a lot. It taught me how to pay attention to an awful lot of things.

So, that would really occupy the years up till about 1950. And the house we were then living in in New Hampshire had been a problem for us; we were unable to keep up payments; we had had a very unhappy event, one of our children had died; so we were emotionally, like they say, anxious to be somewhere else. The continual problem of keeping the property not so much *private* but—there was a pool, a rock pool, a river formed a lovely basin, and it was a lovely place to swim, about the only place that was easily got to for this neighborhood. And we had no problem with the people living *with* us in the sense of the intimate friends or even the acquaintances—but we had this awful business of random tourists. The motels, for instance, began to send people there to swim. So one day I

remember walking down the road and realizing that a travel-
ing carnival had taken all their rubbish and just dumped it in
this woods. That kind of irritation just got frustrating. Any-
how, we were in the mood to leave. And I had met, through a
classmate, like they say, at Harvard, Mitchell Goodman, he's a
novelist, I happened to meet his wife, who was Denise Lever-
tov. They'd gone to live in France on the G.I. Bill that Mitch
could get money from. We were anxious to move and we
thought, well, living in Europe, the basic small income that my
wife had would probably allow us to be more comfortable. So
we went to France on that basis and we lived as neighbors of
the Goodmans, say in fifty, fifty-one—and then they moved
off. We stayed in France for about three years and we had a
very difficult time there. We had hit a time of inflation so that
our money, the availability of what we had to spend, was very
much restricted. We had two children by that time, and a
third child was born there.

Then through the coincidence of little magazines, which is
frankly why we're all here, the coincidence of literary relation-
ships—I came into contact with a young poet, an Englishman,
who had published a poem in a magazine that struck me very
much, not so much in his technique but in the feelings. He
was still using the habitual modes of traditional verse. He was
a man named Martin Seymour Smith. And I wrote to him
care of the magazine to say that poem, you know, was very
interesting and it turned out that he was working as tutor for
Robert Graves' son William in Mallorca. This was a curious
job. William Merwin had been the man who had the job just
before him. Anyhow, we got into correspondence and I would
complain in the letters about the difficulties of living in
France, the kind of unsettledness: there was a great political
criticism of Americans in France at that time. He said, why
don't you come here, and he and his wife then came to pay us
a visit in France, and I sort of returned with them with the
idea that I look over the scene and see where we might live. So
we moved to Mallorca.

Actually the origin of the Divers Press is really due to Mar-
tin because he had a program underway to publish books.
And Martin, like they say, had a mother who was very anxious

to see herself in print. Her actual name was Mrs. Frank Seymour Smith, which was Martin's father, who was one of the most able bookmen for W. H. Smith and Sons in England. He had a knowledge of books as objects; he was neither a critic nor a literary man but he knew books as actual things and had his own concerns with them. But he was very humble about literature. Any man who loves books is humble about literature. But Martin had got involved with the politics of literature. Staying around Graves you do. Graves is very ingenuous in many ways and is, you know, not really very interested in manipulating the possibilities, he certainly wasn't in those years, but at the same time he is very involved with literary activity as *person*. So anyhow we moved to Mallorca and we started this press and I could see very quickly that neither Martin nor myself was going to agree to any sense the other had of what the format, what the look of the book should be. I think we published one, possibly two books—then I split off and my wife and I continued to print books using the Divers Press as a name. I also had the relation now with *Origin*— *Origin* starts 1950, 1951—the first issue is Charles Olson, and happily the second issue, my stories, and so forth.

Sinclair: This is curious to me: how much did you publish before the second issue of *Origin?*

Creeley: I had published in magazines that had no continuity. I mean, they were mostly random. *Wake*, for example, had no continuity. It stopped and then there was nothing that picked up on its occasion. I was writing to Paul Carroll recently, who was reminiscing about *Big Table*. Now *Big Table* picks up on the fact that *Origin* is not being printed further, that the *Black Mountain Review* is starting to peter out, that *Evergreen* is becoming very public. *Big Table* picks up on the impulse of the whole possibility. But then there are magazines—I don't even want to give them names—not that I don't like them, but they're things like *Wings* or *Dedicated* or *Here* (*Here* is actually more interesting; there *is* a magazine called *Here*) but I was published in magazines that I don't like, like *The Window*, or magazines that are continuing because of the persistence of the editor but have no idea of literary continuity. But I think, all told, I could not have published more than a dozen poems. I was writing a lot but I was not publishing. I mean, say a friend says, we'd like some poems, so you send *all* the poems you possess and they take, reasonably, two pages. Then there are the difficulties with the printer and with the money; so if a magazine makes it, it usually comes out six to eight months after your initial intention. And that's because everybody was stuck with the *physical* problem of getting work into print. I can remember Richard Wirtz Emerson and Fred Eckman were editing a magazine called *Golden Goose* which had a continuity, and they printed my first book [*Le Fou*] actually in their series; they also printed Williams' *The Pink Church*, for example. They printed [Norman] Macleod. They were very sympathetic to Patchen. And interested in Pound. They were a contemporary coherence. They took a book of Charles Olson's called *The Praises*. This actually got into proof. Then there was a falling out among them and the book never was printed, never was run off. Then subsequently that book becomes *In Cold Hell, In Thicket*; Cid Corman's *Origin* took over that for its eighth issue and gave the book, which was now changed a bit, that title. But what I'm trying to get to here, is that at this time there is a kind of exploration of these relationships. And they begin to accumulate. A knows B, B knows C, and there begins to be increasing focus. And I think we were curiously lucky that that focus was not literally a question of whether we were all living together or not. You know, people get married and go off about their business; if they have a relationship that depends upon being present to one another, physically, then it's pretty difficult to sustain. Because circumstances lead people to other scenes. But that relationship among those writers who are identified as the *Origin* group never was complicated by a literal geography. Almost all those people were managing their relationships through the mails. That was a time of intense letter writing. For example, I can remember the time that Olson went to Yucatan and the material that I collected then in *Mayan Letters*. And this book must be no more than a fourth or possibly less of the number of letters he was writing.

He used to write so that letters were coming in five times a week. And they were long, you know—

Sinclair: And he was writing to other people all along—

Creeley: Right! He was continually in a process of this kind with everyone. And these were really very intensive statements about what was concerning him then and there. It was sort of an unconscious newsletter of his own concerns. At this same time he was involved with Shakespeare. There's happily a lovely essay as yet unpublished called "Quantity in Verse and Shakespeare's Late Plays." It's going to be collected now in this *Human Universe* volume. It's a lovely demonstration of what he was thinking of and it's an extremely useful piece of writing; he also spoke a lot about what the condition of language was in a *sequence,* call it prose or poetry. So there was Shakespeare, and he was also very involved with the Civil War; he was still involved with the issue both politically and dynamically of the context of the U.S. after the Second World War. You remember he worked for the Democratic Party. He was I think chairman to the foreign language groups represented at the Democratic Convention, during Roosevelt's administration. He comes into that context of persons Roosevelt hired as experts in divers particular disciplines. I mean, I think Roosevelt was the first man to formalize the context of expert advice which was already well known in business. And in the persons that he thus assembled, you have people like Oppenheimer. And you also have Owen Lattimore. I mean, these were persons chosen for their particular experience, rather than their political or social form.

Eichele: When did you start corresponding with Olson?

Creeley: I think it was about 1948 or 1949. I hate to give you an exact date. It follows from Cid: Cid knew Vincent Ferrini, Vincent Ferrini sent some poems to me—we were trying to start a magazine which subsequently was absorbed by *Origin*;

we couldn't get the printing done. We didn't have the money nor the means.

Sinclair: Was there much of a commitment to that activity by that time?

Creeley: Oh, yeah. It's the dissatisfaction with the social occasion of writing. Not that we didn't like it, we didn't have a background for it. You see, aspects of that *kind* of writing and its people do continue very actively in Kenneth Koch's and Frank O'Hara's work on the one hand, or in Donald Hall's work—Hall was also at Harvard—they continued in the *social* situation of writers. Not that they were the less writers, but they had a use of it socially that we didn't have. Bunny Lang's—V. R. Lang's—ability to be so active in the Poets Theater group in Cambridge, is part of her whole *social* situation. I mean, she made, I think, very interesting use of it. But this was a social possibility that writers as myself didn't have. Really we were from the other side of the tracks almost. I remember one time, a classic meeting: I was taken down to a cafe, you know I was still about 26, perhaps 27, and I went down with my gang, I mean I was very humble in my pleasure in being admitted into the group that was centered as *Merlin*. There was Alexander Trocchi, there was Pat Bowles, who interestingly became editor of the *Paris Review*, because Pat Bowles, who was the rough tough kid from South Africa, had the professional ability to edit a magazine. You see now the *Paris Review*, not to castigate them socially, but they were all the kids who went to Harvard who came from good families. These were kids that all moved in a social milieu that did not permit us. So I remember walking into that cafe with Alex and all the dead-end kids of my association and we were sitting down and here across the tables were these, you know, these comfortably and sort of shyly aggressive young men, all of good breeding and manners, who were the editors of the *Paris Review*, with their wives and children sort of making a post–F. Scott Fitzgerald business. Whereas Alex, I remember, used to almost check the arriving boat lists to see what available young American ladies might be found to con into putting money into his magazine. He and the others literally used to sit down (I've been present at such decisions) to decide which among them would be most attractive to the young American who had just wandered into such and such a bar, so that they could con her. And they'd con her in the name of art, as I would con anybody in the name of art, if I could accept my own behavior. In any case, they weren't just going out and lushing; god, it was very severe—I mean these men were *not* self-indulgent. Just witness their activity. They were the first significant publishers of Beckett, for example; they were the first significant publishers in English of Genet. Collection *Merlin*, if you look at the titles, shows the whole foundation of Barney Rosset's subsequent activity.

So in any case, *that* was a happy relationship. This was all happening in the fifties as we began to become identified as active in some literary way, because attention began to come. This had nothing to do with making money or anything. We began to realize ourselves, to get location, to realize what other writers were particular to our own discriminations. Gerhardt in Germany I felt very much for in this sense. In England we were really unable to find anyone; I don't think we ever did at that time. We now begin to. There's a magazine published by Brian Patton, called *Underdog*. There are many magazines. There's *Outburst*, for example, edited by Tom Raworth. And see now the college crowd is beginning to pick up on the possibility, as witness the issues of *Granta*, and even *The Isis* now, begin to show some life.

Sinclair: What about *Prospect*?

Creeley: Yes, *Prospect* is interesting. That's a magazine published at Cambridge, edited by Jeremy Prynne, a teaching fellow, I think, and a very, very good bibliographer and a poet also. But that's a traditional undergraduate magazine that has had a kind of separation from the traditional scene; it's usually picked up by the discontents, you know, as a way of getting hold of something they can think about. That's how that letter to Elaine Feinstein came about; she just wrote Olson and said: what are you doing? And Charles wrote this pretty impressive suggestion of what language might be thought of as doing: something you track in your own experience of it, but also have the possibility of tracking in its own environment as it *has* had an existence. So you test it, as he says, in and out. And words, when they're so received or felt, become really very interesting.

Eichele: Could we turn now to the Black Mountain situation, how you got involved?

Creeley: Let's see. I'm at this point living in Mallorca. And I'm having, like they say, this intensive, continuing correspondence with Olson. *Origin* has now been going on for some years; it's not tired but it's really been carrying a lot of weight for some time. And I think too that we do begin to define our intentions, and some of us begin to feel not a separation but increasing qualification. We become impatient with some of the things done and wish more might be done about others. So we begin to feel there is room for two magazines, not as a criticism at all of Cid's—he is the coherence, always has been—but we begin to think we have enough going for two. And also, Charles was interested—he was now in the position of Rector at Black Mountain—and he was interested to think of some way money might most effectively be used for some activity. That is, the college was now embarrassed in the sense that many, many people were not even aware that it existed, so to hope to get enough students to support its activity was in that way hopeful indeed. We one time literally sat down and figured out with pencil and paper that if we had 35 students we could be self-supporting, and we were unable, we were embarrassed to get 35 students in 1955. So, Charles figured that a magazine—and 35 people are not a large number—a magazine could conceivably get to 35 interested persons.

I was very close to Charles through letters but I had not even met him at the time the *Black Mountain Review* was being planned. So he was involved with *that* business. And he thought, well, if the college published a magazine, this would be the best use of the money available for publicizing itself. That really would effectively distribute the fact that the college was alive; he said, it's like a flag: that's the best way to haul it up. So anyhow, he thereby undertook to get me I think it was about $400 an issue. Or some amount like that. He covered the cost of the issue, in short. We printed four or five hundred copies. And that's the way it happened to be published spring, 1954, from Mallorca. And then there was an attempt to interest people we thought perhaps might be. Paul Goodman had taught at Black Mountain, for example. He said, I don't want to be a contributing editor but I'm sympathetic to what you're doing, and I don't want to take on any concern with what you're doing in a responsible way but I will be willing to help in any other way I can. Kenneth Rexroth did come on as a contributing editor but he was very soon offended because we published two articles: one criticizing Dylan Thomas and the other criticizing Theodore Roethke—and in those days neither man was criticized.

Really we were criticizing the critics of these people; we were criticizing them for making such a structure of assumption about the activity of either of these two men. It was as though Thomas was *only* approachable through this great wash of sentimental regard for his ability to read poems while dead drunk. There's a great love of *that* possibility, the Falstaffian figure. And I thought it became a vulgarization of the whole actuality of his words, of *the* words—they're not his, he didn't make them. And the second thing was that Roethke had become sort of the American Dylan Thomas. Anyhow Kenneth didn't want to be embarrassed in his own associations.

And then Charles invited me to come teach at Black Mountain, which I'd really never considered myself doing. I wasn't a teacher: I didn't know how to teach. But I was desperate to get out of Mallorca so I took him up on it. And boy, with great tentativeness I went. And the persons I met there that first time! I went, actually, twice; I stayed there for perhaps three to four months, then went back to Mallorca, spent almost another year and then returned again—after the breakup of my marriage, and that's best left in the novel. That first time, Mike Rumaker was there; he was very significant for me. Ed Dorn was there; he was significant for me. I felt that these persons were very, *very* interesting indeed. One was primarily a prose writer, the other was writing both prose and poetry and he was such a lovely, resistant *man*—he didn't accept anything on faith; he tested all of his experiences just in order to make sure that he was there too. He didn't want to take it away for himself but he wanted to make sure he had offered it a significant recognition. He never takes things easily. So he was there. And then Charles, of course, was there. It was a lovely company of persons, no matter how difficult the circumstance of survival. And so I found something I had never expected to find: an actual educational organization that was depending upon the authority of its teaching, not on any assumption about that teaching. The college was operated by the faculty. The faculty owned it. The students were completely open; there was very little qualification offered them as to their coming in. There was a very intensive program, but it didn't have the usual formality. It wasn't simply a question of being to class on time, or where is Anthropology 102 meeting this week, or anything of that kind; it was intensely preoccupied with how teaching is accomplished, in all of its aspects. And therefore it came to feel it is much more relevant to have a man who has intimate association with some activity as its possible instructor. Not to tell you the story of my life, but it's much better to be hanging around a blacksmith's shop if you want to learn how to make horseshoes than to be reading books about them.

Sinclair: How about people like Jonathan Williams, Wieners—

Creeley: Jonathan was a student there. I met him actually first in Mallorca. He'd been in the Army. And he came to visit us in Mallorca—but he was known to me, we were known to one another primarily through Black Mountain and Charles. Then John Wieners I remember first meeting at Black Mountain. I've always been deeply touched that John Wieners' first acquaintance with his own possibility as a poet was because Charles read in Boston—I think it was the Trinity Church, which is a sort of old-fashioned church that has civic activities—and Charles for some reason was invited to read there. And it happened that John Wieners was in the audience. He was going to do something else that evening but he just happened to stop in and listen—

Eichele: And he also got a copy of the *Black Mountain Review*—

Creeley: Yes, Charles had copies of *Black Mountain Review #1* that he was passing out. He was *pitching;* I mean he wanted to demonstrate that his college had an active possibility. Anyhow, I happened to be there when John came down for a visit.

Sinclair: He was one of the 35.

Creeley: Yeah. And I drove back to New York with him—well, he was on the way to Boston. Charles and myself and I can't quite remember who else was present, I think there were one or two other people and John and Dana—we drove back in the car. So we had an acquaintance. John was very quiet in those days; he had a lovely sort of tentative manner—he just wanted to look around. He was a very courteous man.

Eichele: What happened as a group to bring these people together who had been carrying on this intense correspondence?

Creeley: That really never *did* happen. That is, all the persons were not ever really together with one another. I remember in Vancouver a couple of years ago, Charles or Robert or somebody said, gee, this is the first time that we've all been together. It was really the first time in our lives that the three of us were present at the same time. In other words, Robert had spent a short period in Mallorca; I'd met him there first, he'd come over—through *Origin* we were known to each other. Robert had wanted to be in Mallorca, he wrote me because he knew it was cheap to live there, and we helped him find a house. Denise and I had been together both in the States and in France; Paul and I had known each other in New York; Paul came to Mallorca. Olson I'd known at Black Mountain. But I mean we *weren't* a nucleus geographically ever. Although Robert also taught at Black Mountain he came, I think, literally when I left. The second time. He stayed on till the college finished. Or at least had to close because of lack of money. But it's almost more interesting to demonstrate that the *place* can be as viable as this then was, that this activity of coming and going is relevant to education also because what contemporary education is facing is the problem that it has an increasingly static or unwieldy *location*. Colleges can't be *put* in the country; they can't be *put* in the city. You've demonstrated that a college occurs—I'm thinking, John and Robin, of your own activity with the Artist's Workshop—you're demonstrating that a college occurs at any point that this concern of how do you measure, how is value possible, how do you have the use of yourself in what activity you do—any time this is admitted as a context a college occurs. It's what Alex Trocchi is now talking about with his sense of *spontaneous university.* Now see this is really a dilemma because I remember visiting at Michigan State and talking to various friends there, people I'd met there, and they said, the courses aren't really the problem— the actual physical organization of the place is almost overwhelming: 35,000 students and we're not worried about who will teach Beowulf, we're worried about how do you keep that plumbing from breaking down. This kind of problem is immense, really immense indeed—literally so.

But this college that we had in mind was as viable and as momentary and as moving as the fact that people moved around in their lives. The different attentions at different moments in time. So it was a place to *go.* It really was that place we were talking about apropos this conference: a place to go sit down when you wanted to. And we weren't limited: people were always drifting through, coming back, coming for the first time. And the very form that Olson insisted upon for his own teaching there when he first came to Black Mountain was that he would come down at the end of each month and stay perhaps four or five days and work intensively with people, then go back to Washington where he'd been living and go about his own business; I mean he not only knew, he realized entirely that you don't get anything from someone who's not given time to be active; you can't get anything from a painter who's prepared to sit in a classroom talking *about* painting all day. He's just not going to be able to do the thing. You certainly can't find out anything from a man who's active in some context if he's not given the opportunity of doing what he literally can do.

With Linda Wagner

Linda Wagner was certainly a friend. We met first when she and her husband came to the Vancouver Poetry Conference mentioned earlier, and we continued to keep in touch as she worked on her W. C. Williams book and then another on Denise Levertov. I recall a somewhat painful photograph she once showed me, of herself and Williams, taken during one of her visits to talk with him about her study of his work. She sits there in a charmingly vivid red dress, clearly bursting with pride and pleasure, given the circumstance. Equally clearly he sits, battered by his recent strokes, looking markedly tired and distracted. But how can one begrudge that delight?

Now reading, I'm struck by what our talking emphasizes as politi-cal, how that time so particularized all our definitions of person, including writers, as necessarily a part of a common social world of others. So one felt strongly about the possible coercion of federal grants, for example. Later I applied for and got an N.E.A. grant without qualms, though I wondered if I had simply grown quiescent. The sixties were a time of profoundly literal questioning, not only of the ways and means of an art but, far more importantly, of the social and spiritual factors informing all. I had an excellent ear for my attempt to get things straight in my own mind.

In fact, Linda's care here is simple evidence of the whole nature of her work as a scholar, which has never presumed upon nor overridden its "subjects." Ours was a great occasion for me in particular, just that this was to be the basis of an interview for the Paris Review, *which felt to me like substantial progress. So we were if anything serious indeed, Linda with her charming emphasis upon the "literary," me with my sternly determined answers. One forgets, I suppose, just how formidable such a circumstance seems when it's happening. To be included in "The Art of Poetry" series was, in my imagination, the big time. Anyhow, the following ruminations appeared (in revised form) in the fall of 1968 issue (vol. X, no. 44: 18).*

Wagner: You have said that poetry is "the basic act of speech, of utterance." Are you implying that self-expression is the poet's motivation, or is there more to be said about his desire to communicate, his interest in possible readers?

Creeley: I don't think that "possible readers" are really the context in which poetry is written. For myself it's never been the case. I'm looking for something I can say—I'm not looking for a job or an easy solution to problems—but I'm given to write as I can and in that act I use whatever I can to gain the articulation that seems to me called for. And I certainly will pay no attention to possible readers insofar as they may not respond to what I've offered in this way. I have found, for example, that the poems I wrote in the fifties, which at that time had only the sympathetic reading of friends, that those poems have gained the audience here implied, not because I intended it but simply because I have gained them—but I could never have anticipated that. If one in that way plays to the gallery, I think it's extraordinarily distracting. The whole performance of writing then becomes some sort of odd entertainment of persons one never meets and probably would be embarrassed to meet in any case. So I'm only interested in what I can articulate with the things given me as confrontation. I can't worry about what it costs me. I don't think any man writing can worry about what the act of writing costs him, even though at times he is very aware of it. Again, when Stendhal dedicated his work in effect to readers who would be alive—in say 1930, 1935, a hundred years later—he recognized the political and social circumstances that would make him politically suspect; so that he obviously wrote for the sheer pleasure and relief of the articulation so to be gained. And I would say, I do too.

Wagner: Communication *per se*, then, isn't a primary motive for the poet?

Creeley: It is for some; for others, it isn't. It depends on what is meant by communication, of course. I, for example, would be very much cheered to realize that someone had felt what I had been feeling in writing—I would be very much reassured that someone had felt with me in that writing. Yet this can't be the context of my own writing. When I come to write, I frankly cannot be distracted by what people are going to think of what I'm writing. Later I may have horrible doubts indeed as to what it is and whether or not it will ever be read with this kind of response by other persons, but it can never enter importantly into my writing.

So I cannot say that communication in the sense of telling someone is what I'm engaged with. In writing I'm telling something to myself, curiously, that I didn't have the knowing of previously. One time, again some years ago, Franz Kline was being questioned—not with hostility but with intensity, by another friend—and finally he said, "Well, look, if I paint what *you* know, then that will simply bore you, the repetition from me to you. If I paint what I know, it will be boring to myself. Therefore I paint what I *don't* know." And I write what I don't know, in that sense.

Communication, then, is a word one would have to spend much time defining. One question I have—doesn't all speech imply that one is speaking with what is known, is possible of discovery? "Can you tell someone something he doesn't know?" has always been a question in my own mind. And if it is true that you cannot tell someone something "new," then the act of reading is that one is reading *with* someone. And I feel that when people read my poems most sympathetically, they are reading with me as I am writing with them. So communication this way is mutual feeling with someone, not a didactic process of information.

Wagner: I have increasingly felt that to some poets—Allen Ginsberg, William Carlos Williams, yourself—this being read *with*, sympathetically, was very important.

Creeley: There are many, many ways of feeling in the world, and many qualifications of that feeling. At times in my own life I've been embarrassed to feel I had a significant relationship with other people—that is, I felt that my world was extraordinarily narrow and egocentric and possible only to some self-defined importance. So that reading in that sense I've just spoken of—that sympathetic being with—has always been an important possibility for me. What Robert Duncan calls the ideal reader has always been someone I've thought of—but not *in* writing, *after* it.

Wagner: One question that's fairly relevant here might be this issue of using so-called prose rhythms in poetry, of taking the language of poetry from natural speech. How does the poet himself decide what is poetry and what is conversation? And are they as close as the theory seems to indicate?

Creeley: If we think of Louis Zukofsky's poetics as being "a function with upper limit music and lower limit, speech," perhaps that will help to clarify what the distinctions are. Really, the organization of poetry has moved to a further articulation in which the rhythmic and sound structure now becomes not only evident but a primary coherence in the total organization of what's being experienced. In conversation, you see, this is not necessarily the case. It largely isn't, although people speaking (at least in American speech) do exhibit clusters or this isochronous pattern of phrase groups with one primary stress; so there is a continuing rhythmic insistence in conversation. But this possibility has been increased in poetry so that now the rhythmic and sound organization have been given a very marked emphasis in the whole content. Prose rhythms in poetry are simply one further possibility of articulating pace; these so-called prose rhythms tend to be slower so that therefore they give perhaps a useful drag.

I would like to make the point that it isn't that poets are using "common" words or a common vocabulary. This kind of commonness is deceptive. For example, if one reads Williams carefully, he finds that the words are *not* largely common. What is common is the *mode* of address, the way of speaking that's commonly met with in conversations. But when that occurs in poetry, already there's a shift that is significant: that fact in a poem is very distinct from that fact in conversation. And I think what really was gained from that sense of source in common speech was the recognition that the intimate knowing of a way of speaking—such as is gained as Olson says with mother's milk—what's gained in that way offers the kind of intensity that poetry peculiarly admits.

These words known from one's childhood have the most intense possibility for the person writing. Whatever language is removed from that source goes into an ambivalence that is at times most awkward. Now a very accomplished man—say Duncan—can both attempt and succeed in a rhetorical mode that's apart from this context, although it may well *not* be; yet Duncan's virtue is that he can move from one to the other with such skill and ease. As in "Two Presentations," he moves to the immediate context of speech (literally, to quotation) yet gathers it into a mode of rhetoric that is the basic speech pattern of the whole poem. In other words, it isn't simply an imitation of common ways of speaking, it's rather a recognition that the intimate senses of rhythm and sound will be gained from what one knows in this way.

Wagner: You have written recently that it is not the single word choices so much as it is the sound and rhythm of entire passages that determines the immediacy of the language. Is that concept relevant to this discussion?

Creeley: In conversation with Basil Bunting last fall, he said that his own grasp of what poetry might be for him was first gained when he recognized that the sounds occurring in a poem could carry the emotional content of the poem as ably as anything "said." That is, the modifications of sounds—and the modulations—could carry this emotional content. He said further, that whereas the lyric gives such an incisive and intense singularity, usually, to each word that is used in a longer poem such as his own "The Spoils," there's an accumulation that can occur much more gradually so that sounds are built up in sustaining passages and are not, say, given an individual presence but accumulate that presence as a totality. So that one is not aware, let us say, that the word *the* is carrying its particular content, but as that *e* sound or *th* sound accumulates, it begins to exert an emotional effect that is gained not by any insistence on itself as singular word but as accumulation. To quote Pound again, "Prosody consists of the total articulation of the sound in a poem"—and that's what I'm really talking about.

Wagner: Is line and stanza arrangement still used to indicate what the poet intends, rhythmically? Are poets today more concerned with the sound or with the visual appearance *per se* of their work?

Creeley: For myself, lines and stanzas indicate my rhythmic intention. I don't feel that any poet of my acquaintance whose work I respect is working primarily with the visual appearances except for Ian Finlay, and in Finlay's case he is working in a very definite context of language which has to do with the fact that there have been *printed* words for now, say, 400 years. The experience of words as printed has provided a whole possibility of that order as visual as opposed to oral or audible. Ian's working in the context of language as what one sees on signboards, stop signs, titles of books—where the words *are* in that sense; and there is an increasing school of poets who are involved with concrete poetry in that way. But for myself the typographical context of poetry is still simply the issue of how to score—in the musical sense—to indicate how I want the poem to be read.

Wagner: I have noticed in your own readings that you pause after each line, even though many of the lines are very short. You're not just creating quatrains of fairly even shape, then?

Creeley: No, I tend to pause after each line, a slight pause. Those terminal endings give me a way of both syncopating and indicating a rhythmic measure. I think of those lines as something akin to the bar in music—they state the rhythmic modality. They indicate what the base rhythm of the poem is, hopefully, to be.

The quatrain to me is operating somewhat like the paragraph in prose. It is both a semantic measure and a rhythmic measure. It's the full unit of the latter. I remember Pound in a letter one time saying, "Verse consists of a constant and a variant." The quatrain for me is the constant. The variant then can occur in the line, but the base rhythm also has a constant which the quatrain in its totality indicates. I wanted something stable, and the quatrain offered it to me; as earlier the couplet form had. This, then, allows all the variability of what could be both said and indicated as rhythmic measure.

Wagner: Where in this whole discussion does your often-quoted statement, "Form is never more than an extension of content," fall?

Creeley: Olson had lifted that statement from a letter I had written him, and I'm very sure it was my restatement of something that he had made clear to me. It's not at all a new idea. I find it in many people, prose writers as well as poets—Flaubert, for example. I would now almost amend the statement to say, "Form is what happens." It's the fact of things in the world, however they are. So that form in that way is simply the presence of any thing.

What I was trying then to make clear was that I felt that form—if removed from that kind of intimacy—became something static and assumptional. I felt that the way a thing was said would intimately declare *what* was being said, and so therefore, form was never more than an extension of what it was saying. The what of what was being said gained the how of what was being said, and the how (the mode) then became what I called "form." I would again refer the whole question to Olson's "Projective Verse." It's the attempt to find the intimate form of what's being stated as it is being stated. A few weeks ago I was moved to hear Hans Morgenthau in the teach-in which was televised saying, "Facts have their own dynamic." Which is to say something in one way akin—content has its own form.

Wagner: Some people use the term "organic" poem to refer to one in which this principle of form applies. How does the organic poem differ from what is usually called the "traditional" poem?

Creeley: The traditional poem is after all the historical memory of a way of writing that's regarded as being significant. And I'm sure again that all those poems were once otherwise—as Stendhal feels, Racine *was* modern at the time Racine was writing those plays. But then for his work to be respected in the nineteenth century as being *the* way of writing—this, of course, was something else again. This is a respect merely for the thing that has happened not because it is still happening but because it did happen. That I find suspect. If one is respecting something that continues to happen, as with Shakespeare, then I agree. But if one respects a thing that isn't happening anymore, that is now so removed by its diffusion into historical perspective, then of course "traditional" becomes a drag indeed. But the traditional is, after all, the cumulative process of response. It has its uses without question. But it can only be admitted as the contemporary can respond to it.

Wagner: What of the modern poets who write in sonnets, quatrains, blank verse? Can they still be using the organic rationale?

Creeley: Certainly, if these forms can occur. If they offer possibility of articulation, then of course they can be used. Valéry, for example, in *The Art of Poetry* makes some very astute comments about his own methods of working, and he found these forms in this "formal" sense to be very useful to him insofar as they provoked him to extraordinary excitement and to extraordinary ability. He loved the problem of them. Now you see, each according to his nature again, to quote from Pound's quote of the Confucian text. There's no rule. Only when sonnets become descriptive of values that are questionable, do I find them offensive. But I don't think they are *per se* to be written off, except that they are highly difficult now to use because society does not offer them a context with which they are intimate, anymore than society offers a context for dancing the gavotte.

Wagner: A side issue here, perhaps. Does an artist's "sincerity" have any influence on the quality of his work? Can a poet write good poems about a subject if he has no feeling about it?

Creeley: I don't see how. If one respects Pound's measure of "Only emotion endures" and "Nothing counts save the quality of the affection," then having no feelings about something seems to prohibit the possibility of that kind of quality entering. At the same time, there are many ways of feeling about things; and it may be that—as in the case of poems by Ted Berrigan— one is feeling about the fact that there is no attachment of subjective feeling to the words. It's a very subtle question.

I remember one time Irving Layton wrote a very moving poem, "Elegy for Fred Smith." Later, Gael Turnbull, very impressed by the poem, said to him, "You must feel very badly that your friend has died, and your poem concerning this fact is very, very moving." And Irving then explained that there was no man named Smith; he simply wanted to write this kind of poem. But you see, he wanted the feeling too; he wanted to gain the way one might feel in confronting such a possibility. There wasn't, as it happened, a real fact that provoked this poem, but there was certainly a feeling involved. And it was certainly a "subject" that Irving had "feeling" about.

This issue of sincerity in itself, however, can be a kind of refuge of fools. I am sure that Goldwater was sincere in certain ways, and I don't think that that necessarily protects him from a judgment that's hostile to his intent. But it will gain him a hearing, as it obviously did. The zealot is often sincere. In other words, sincerity as a quality is one thing—well, I'd simply point to Louis Zukofsky's discussion of sincerity in his notes for the Objectivist issue of *Poetry* in 1931. But I'm going to take sincerity in my own reference which again goes back to Pound, that ideogram that he notes: man standing by his word. *That* kind of sincerity has always been important to me and is another measure of my own commitment to what I'm doing.

Wagner: No doubt there are pitfalls, too. Eddie Guest was probably as sincere as anyone writing today. Why wasn't Guest a Williams?

Creeley: Again, you see, we have an easy answer. If we do believe that "Nothing counts save the quality of the affection," then we have an easy measure for qualifying Guest—the "affection" in Guest is of very poor quality. It's so generally articulated and so blurred with assumptional sentiment that it's a kind of mess. It's too general. So that would be the difference between him, I would feel, and someone like Williams who has that virtue of a much more complex and intimate and modulated quality of feeling—and is much more articulate in the area of that feeling, and not only gives evidence of it, but allows its evidence to be felt by the reader.

Wagner: Let's move to a little different issue now, although in a way, I suppose this is still sincerity in a larger sense. Recent happenings have made many of us question what actually is the artist's responsibility to his culture: Lowell's refusal to attend the White House Culture-fest, the Artists' and Writers' Protest against policies in Vietnam—what *should* the artist be doing politically?

Creeley: Well, it's impossible that a man should be only a "fact" in himself. I suppose what Robert Lowell was saying was, among other things that he simply didn't want to be part of a group of people who were not only admitting but making use of a social occasion that was also a demonstration of commitment to a way of thinking that he himself found very suspect. I know that many of my fellow writers, for example, Allen Ginsberg, Charles Olson, and Robert Duncan in his recent poems (*Passages*) have undertaken a very direct involvement with contemporary political events—as Duncan's poem called "The Multiversity" and the two or three poems that follow it in that cycle show. These are very abrupt and highly articulate attacks upon modern political contexts, that is, literally on Johnson and the administration; also upon the circumstance at the University of California in Berkeley and the Free Speech Movement.

Wagner: Today's artist should not be an ivory-tower iconoclast, then?

Creeley: No. It's impossible that one should be indifferent to what qualifies him in the world. That is, my ability to live and make a living and secure the possibility of family for myself— this is political. Its *polis* is the fact of people living together in some common place and time, as an organization of people. And all that relates to it is a large part of life indeed. So that I can no more avoid political concerns than I can avoid the fact that it's raining outside.

Now what I'm going to do about it is a question intimate to my own nature and decisions involved with that nature. I have, for example, joined in the protest that you mention. And in my conduct both as a teacher and as a writer, I would like to think that any time these concerns confront me I am not only prepared, in some specious sense, but I feel that there is only the answer that I must say what I feel—that is, that the Vietnam conflict called war is an obscene invasion of both American and Vietnamese life, and that it is in that sense a moral evil that I cannot support in any sense whatsoever. I will lend whatever time and support I can give to a protest. But I also remember, because I'm not often able to involve a political context in my writing, that I felt a kind of dismay that I was being irresponsible. But then I frankly have used as a reassurance a statement that Williams made some time ago (early fifties) on receiving the National Book Award.

It goes something like this. "In dreams, as the poet W. B. Yeats has told us, begin responsibilities. The government of the words is our responsibility since it is of all governments the archetype." And then he notes the fact that in this conduct of words many poets have as a result been killed outright or driven into exile. That is, language is a political act. Anything that enters into the world as decision of this order involves the political context.

So that I have felt that if in my own conduct as a writer, I could both propose this kind of commitment I referred to earlier as a man standing by his word; and if I would not be blocked or shamed or coerced (as Allen Ginsberg would say) out of my natural skin, that was possibly my contribution to the political reality of the time in which I lived. That is, if I would stand by what I felt to be existent in the world and demonstrate its reality as best I could, this possibly gained for me a political term of responsibility.

I would hate, however, to confuse these things with what one can call "topicality." That is, I am dismayed that so soon after the assassination of President Kennedy there was a proposal by two men, very sincere and well-meaning in their suggestion— in any case, they were put to work editing a collection of poems on the death of President Kennedy. And I questioned that, when I got their letter. I said first of all, which was probably the real fact, that I had no poems that were involved directly with his death and therefore couldn't contribute; but further, that I thought they were making capital so to speak of an event that was much more profound in its implications than this kind of use of it would frankly admit. I felt they were rushing this thing into print almost too conveniently.

You see, we're back again to Williams' sense of the government of the words as our responsibility. What outrages the articulation of feeling in language, what makes language subverted to the meager reality of distorted and finally criminal acts against men such as are evident in this circumstance— what distorts and beguiles and coerces by means of language can only, I think, be confronted by a use of language which makes obvious that criminal distortion on the part of those who make use of it. In other words, it's impossible to either ignore or to separate oneself from such a circumstance. It means for me personally that language must be more insistent in its articulations than ever, must be more articulate in all ways, so as not to lose the possibility of saying what one feels in a world which has been given such assumptions that at times it's a nightmare to think how to confront them with sufficient energy and definition, to embarrass them in their own place.

Wagner: In return for this concern, then, should there be any state or federal responsibility to the arts?

Creeley: I feel, no. I have never wanted the patronage personally of any state or federal government. I feel that it's a very great danger. Allen Ginsberg, for example, reporting his conversations with Yevtushenko and the other poets in Russia recently, said that one of the largest dilemmas they have concerning the circumstances of American writers is the fact that American writers seem to work outside of the structure of the government they have. Not that they are indifferent to that structure but that they work apart from it. The state in Russia, Allen was saying and these persons made evident, is such an admitted fact that it is impossible for them to think any articulation can occur apart from its structure. Yevtushenko, for example, had just written a very long poem, and then was asked by the censors to make some four hundred corrections. Now he did that because, for him, it's impossible to think of how a poem can occur in his situation without being subject to this limit.

That is, remembering as Olson says, that "limits are what any of us are inside of," for the Russian poet, the state is literally one of those limits which he both respects and accepts. It isn't that he is a "Communist" or anything of that sort so simply, but that he admits this as a real condition of his existence. In order to say anything, he will admit the fact that it must be said in the context of that structure. In this country, you see, we don't have such a total involvement with the government in relation to the people who are living with that government, so we don't have this context. And I would be suspicious of anything that promoted it without full understanding on the part of all involved. I have rather a Thoreau sense of not wanting to belong to any club that I have not chosen to join, which I think is a pretty American insistence.

I have seen, in some sense, what happens when state or federal agencies enter into the context of the university or college. For example, the National Defense Educational Act—scholarships funds and whatever offered to students by the government—has really been a problematic help. It commits the students to saying, as I understand it, that they will never be "Communist," and this, to propose this to someone 18 or 19 or whatever age, is an awfully difficult thing indeed. How do they know that? And then they'll become legally responsible if at any time in their later life they choose this as an identity for themselves. In other words, it's an act which has really created great difficulty. It's a very, very loaded help which, I understand, Eisenhower was critical of, that is, critical of the wording. No, I don't want state or federal responsibility to the arts. I think if they keep the roads paved and provide schools with operating funds, and Medicare, and such things as that, then that is enough for the moment.

In the paper a day ago there was a note about Johnson's quotation of what he thought was a poem of Lowell's which turned out to be a quotation from "Dover Beach" by Matthew Arnold. In other words, I've never felt that the distinctions which would be possible to government persons would be of much interest. I think that's perhaps why the Library of Congress, despite its sympathy often to artists, has never been an active force in the arts; and why the Poetry Consultant at the Library has never been an active force during the times of his occupancy of the chair. Williams' fate in his appointment, for example, is too often what happens; and I was interested to hear a discussion of this last fall in England by Cleanth Brooks. Both Brooks and Leonie Adams were Fellows of the Library, and tried very hard to have Williams reinstated, according to Brooks, but the point was that the government agency is apparently much too ponderous, too intent upon its own structure, ever to admit the fact that the arts must have a much more fluid condition in which to function.

Wagner: Without government assistance, what is, the financial answer for today's artists? How can the poet support himself and his family, and still have adequate time to write? You have taught in various colleges; do you feel that teaching is compatible with writing?

Creeley: I've known so many people with so many various jobs who were writing that I don't think there's any one answer. I was listening to a discussion recently in which it was pointed out that Ives, after all, was a very wealthy man and that his music is certainly very significant; yet that some other composer might be poor indeed. In short, the conditions for writing aren't so simply defined. Each man makes whatever solution is possible. I've found myself often embarrassed by the fact that I do have time provided for me, as by grants; then

I'm almost shut up. Simply having the time designated as time "in which to write" seems to make that writing impossible. This is not a plea not to be given such grants, because I have other uses for them which are very happy; and I feel that the rest and the accumulation of things that they make possible is very useful to me. But no, I am living as I find I can, and I assume all other people do the same thing. Some can't; then it's a question of who can help, but there's no easy solution.

Poets have been so many kinds of persons that there is no one solution that will apply to even three of them. They've been so many things. As we know of Williams in his own life, being a doctor obviously was of great importance to him. I don't know what being an insurance executive meant to Wallace Stevens but it apparently gave him the possibilities he was after. On the other hand, someone like Lew Welch, whom I met recently in San Francisco—the jobs he's done in his life have been important to him: working on fishing boats or as lookout in national forests. Each man comes to the solution. I find for my own case that teaching is compatible with writing; it gives me a way of living in the world. It earns me the living I need, and it's an activity that I can respect. No matter how often I find individual instances that I don't respect, it gives me an active voice in something I can respect myself in doing. So that it's compatible with writing in that it lets me find the world, and it allows me admission to a world that's constantly coming into being—that is, as I understand it, as of next year fifty percent of the population of this country will be 25 years old or younger. Many of those people are in colleges or univerities; that is the context for their activities, as evidence the Free Speech Movement in Berkeley. So it's a very interesting place to be now.

Wagner: We hear frequently that this is an excellent period for poetry, that from all the present experimentation will come strong new modes. As a poet, do you feel as if these are peak years?

Creeley: I don't feel so simply that these are "peak years." I know I feel that we have been party to an extraordinary experimentation and a building on the possibilities offered by Ezra Pound, William Carlos Williams, and, earlier, Whitman—I think that this last ten or fifteen years in American poetry has been perhaps the most rich of any, or certainly will prove to be as rich as those in the earlier part of the century. What's now happening is something else again; I find that there's an extraordinary interest in poetry, and certainly many, many people writing it—but I've as yet not seen, except in a few instances, a clear significance of its effect. For example, recently in San Francisco at the Berkeley Poetry Conference, I was very interested in the poems of Ted Berrigan. Now they come from a mode that has been developed partly by Frank O'Hara, more by John Ashbery, and perhaps even more significantly by Jackson Mac Low. In Berrigan's poems, words are returned to an almost primal circumstance, by a technique that makes use of feedback, that is, a repetitive relocation of phrasing, where words are curiously returned to an almost objective state of presence so that *they* speak rather than someone speaking with them. It is something that Gertrude Stein had been concerned with. But these people presently are using it for a most interesting possibility, and I'm interested in that sense in what they are doing, very much so. I feel that this is probably one of the most interesting new possibilities in writing to have occurred in some time. Otherwise, I think that there is the usual activity, but I don't really find much distinction in it. I do not mean to criticize those persons now writing, but—this may be simply an instance of my own age at this point. I feel that these are peak years, however, in regard to the demand that society now makes upon poetry. That demand has never been more insistent. Therefore, let's say the occasion is certainly here. The time is right, in all possible senses. At the same time, perhaps the very wealth of possibilities is itself a slight confusion to people trying to decide which of many things is that most akin to their own circumstance.

But I feel that for myself these are peak years indeed. I have everything I want, for example. I think most poets writing must feel somewhat the same, that there's no reason to sit and grouch about not having something because—my god—

there's incredible amount of possibility in all senses. Again, what I did find out in Germany was this, that German poets and prose writers also are very interested in what they call "the American vernacular." That is, we are blessed by having a literary language which makes use of the so-called vernacular as easily as it does the so-called literary. We can use either a highly developed rhetorical mode or else we can use a very commonly situated vernacular. And we have no diminishment of the literary possibility in either case.

Wagner: In Germany, then, that's not so?

Creeley: No, there the language of poetry has been primarily a literary language so that poets like Enzensberger and others have been interested to translate poets as Williams simply that they find in Williams this vernacular in such intensity that they hope by translation to gain its use, in the German context. So that there, you see, the modes are much more limited at present. Also, then, that's even more true in the case of France, where poetic language has really so limited the articulation possible to poetry. I was talking to Claude Gallimard about whether or not there were many French poets of interest, and the only one he really remarked upon was, unhappily, a young poet whose name I cannot remember—a Belgian, I think, significantly enough. He was then about eighteen. But he was the *only* one they really had come upon. In this country, it's possible to find at least ten or fifteen persons who are writing with extraordinary qualification.

Wagner: Would you consider them major poets? In other words, have these strong new modes appeared?

Creeley: Yes, they've appeared. Pound has given so many possibilities just in his work that it will be a long time indeed before they're exhausted. I feel that Pound will take his place in the context of literature in the same way that Chaucer did, in offering the possibility of iambic pentameter or actually the iamb as a measure for verse. In other words, setting a mode in the technical performance of the craft that stays for all the time subsequent. Or Spenser, in his modulations or inventions, would be another figure. Basil Bunting is right I think when he makes a parallel between Pound and Spenser as being two great innovators in the art of poetry, whose work may then be built upon for years and years. So that I think that these modes coming, both from such men as Pound and Williams, and from more contemporary figures like Charles Olson—that the modes are evident and that now their particular use is really up to the qualification of each person who attempts to make use of them.

Wagner: Perhaps we should continue into the big questions. Talking about "strong modes," what in your estimation is a strong, or a good, poem?

Creeley: Well, a good poem ... I've come in the past few months at least—whether from fatigue or from a kind of ultimately necessary conservatism—to feel that there can be at least one kind of primary measure for the activity of poetry; and perhaps this statement will seem oblique, but in any case what has really stuck in my head through the years as a measure of literature are the two statements of Pound's which I mentioned earlier: "Only emotion endures," and "Nothing counts save the quality of the affection." Now these offer to me two precise terms of measure for what the possibility of a poem can be. I don't feel that what the poem says in a didactic or a semantic sense—although this fact may be very important indeed—I don't feel that this is what a poem is about primarily; I don't think this is its primary fact. I feel rather it is that complex of emotion evident by means of the poem, or by the response offered in terms of that emotion so experienced, that is the most signal characteristic that a poem possesses. So, I feel that the measure of poetry is that emotion which it offers, and that, further, the quality of the articulation of that emotion—how it is felt, the fineness of its articulation, then—is the further measure of its reality.

And to that, then, I would add two things. One, the sense of poetry that's evident in Williams' introduction to *The Wedge* (1944) when he says, "When a man makes a poem, *makes* it, mind you," so that it has "an intrinsic movement of its own to verify its authenticity"—in other words, so that it is not simply a wish on the part of the writer (or not simply a communication, saying "I'm telling you this"), but has within it all that it needs to survive in its own statement. This, I feel, is a necessary condition for a poem that's active.

For one last sort of sense of measure, apropos how a poem is, I would take Zukofsky's point that one enjoys poetry with reference to the pleasure it offers as sight, sound, and intellection. These would offer for me three primary conditions of a poem's activity. And I would much respect them. From all of this—I can't answer such a question directly because I don't think it's a case of having an absolute measure that defines an absolute poem. I simply use these senses of poetry in my own approach, in reading. I don't do it at all consciously, but when I have read and have been moved or engaged by a poem, very often I realize that this is the *why* of the circumstance. This is how it has happened.

Wagner: Would your answer be any different had I said a good *contemporary* poem?

Creeley: No, it wouldn't be. I have no interest in *contemporary* as a sense of *the latest*. I remember reading years ago in the work of a linguist, Joshua Whatmough, a very simple book called *Language*, his comment that poetry had said nothing different for the last 6,000 years. And perhaps now that we can go back farther in time, we will find that poetry has not said anything so different in the past 20,000 or 30,000 years. As Zukofsky suggests, its concerns have always been war, the love between man and woman or man and man, friendship. And then the seasons and the insistent change they make manifest. And, finally, the care of the earth, the literal experience of being able to live in a physical place. They have been a curiously insistent set of themes. I don't know, war is the most intense and perhaps the largest political possibility ever experienced by men; and then the most intimate measure of his life is his love for woman or that of woman for man, man for man. So that it is here, at least, contemporaries can relate.

I would use the word *contemporary* in Stendhal's sense of it. (I might say that Stendhal is probably the one writer whom I've had consistent regard for since I was reading anything at all. I'm just now rereading some of his work, and I'm struck again by the incredible clarity and fluidity of his thinking.) That is, it's necessary to articulate these kinds of possibilities in the intimate language of one's own reality. That is to be modern, he felt. To borrow the language of other times and places when it is not intimate is to risk faking—even though one be very sincere. It is like making old furniture. Even though the piece may be an exact replica, the situation of the authentic is always particular. When that aspect of time and place is removed from it, it becomes a curiously vacant thing. So I don't think that I would have spoken differently of a good contemporary poem, because a poem that is active in these ways that I've tried to suggest is always active in these ways, if it can be understood at all. Its language may simply be lost to us by some effect of time or a shift in the dialect, where we have lost the ability to read, of course. But, that aside, I would feel that a poem is continually active and that time, in the historical sense, is of no interest in a measure of the poem's activity.

Wagner: Generally speaking, do you think that the criterion of "meaning" is important to most modern poets? I was reading the other day a poem by Gary Snyder, "How to Make Stew in the Pinacate Desert": " . . . Now put in the strips of bacon. / In another pan have all the vegetables cleaned up and peeled and sliced. / Cut the beef shank meat up small . . . ." I'm going to be argumentative here and ask, if technique is the rationale for Snyder's poem, have we gone too far with the emphasis on technique?

Creeley: I was struck by a definition of "meaning" that Olson offered at the Berkeley Conference. He said simply, "That which exists through itself is what is called meaning." That kind of meaning, that kind of signification, is what a poem is. It *does* so exist through itself, through agency of its own activity; therefore, is; therefore, has meaning. What a poem says as some kind of instruction that can be understood and then thrown away—I find this kind of meaning to be very secondary, to be finally *not* that which qualifies poetry in the active manner.

About Snyder's poem. The context of the poem is very relevant; I perhaps know too much about it. For example, it is addressed to two friends. What Gary's here doing is literally giving them a recipe for stew, but—*and*, rather—his way of speaking is evident. A tone or a mode or a kind of speech is occurring. Yes, you can literally take this poem as a recipe for how to make stew, but in this way of saying something there's also an emotional context, a kind of feeling. That, to my mind, is the significant part of this poem. It's the kind of address and the kind of feeling that's engendered by it; and it's the way the words go in that way that is to me the most intimate aspect of this poem as poem.

Now, what can we call it? Technique? Sure, there's technique in that the poem is articulated and held, in the way the words are placed in lines. There's a speed offered in the way the line is going there. But I don't think that he has gone too far, any more than I felt that the actual record of drilling that occurs in Williams' *Paterson* was going too far. It seemed to be very prosaic, but it gave an extraordinary sense of how far one did have to dig down to find what was intimate, vital, and living in relation to one's own needs. Just as the water was only to be found after having gone through all those levels, the very character of that report gave a real sense of what it is like to try to find something living in an environment that is so covered, so much the accumulation of refuse, and waste, and tedium, and misuse. So that I would rather not in that way talk of "technique" as something extensible or separate from the actual circumstance. And I would have respect for this particular poem of Gary's. Again I fall back on Pound's "Only emotion endures." This particular emotion is of an address to friends meant as a warmth which all three shall share, therefore anyone. In that possibility I find the most interest.

Of course I'm interested in how he did it, but I don't feel that he has gone too far with technique. It's very simple indeed; it's primarily blank verse, and that's been evident for many years. One could go to Milton and find much instruction for writing it.

Wagner: You are one of the few modern poets, Bob, to escape the charge of "all means and no matter." Did you—do you—consciously choose your subjects?

Creeley: Never that I've been aware of. I may make too much emphasis upon that, but I can't remember ever setting out to write a poem literally about something that I was conscious of before I began to write. Again I fall back on Williams' sense which I may misquote. It's in the *Autobiography*, where he says in answer to the very usual charge of his lack of profundity that dogged him all during the forties and into the fifties (that was when he was being attacked for being involved with "nonpoetic" subjects and for things which were "trivial," etc., etc.,—again, you see, that's what "meaning" in the secondary sense can land on someone. It seems to qualify them as being specious or insignificant. In other words, if the meaning in this secondary manner is not addressed to something that seems very ponderous indeed, then the man writing is charged with being "unprofound." It's a very, very silly way to think of poems, and I suppose that what has come to correct that "meaning" is something partly akin to haiku where it's very evident that a few words indeed about extraordinarily common things or sights or feelings can provoke an endless wave of emotion, as long as it's held in mind). But in any case, Williams says, "The poet thinks with his poem. In that lies his thought, and that in itself is the profundity."

For myself, writing has always been the way of finding what I was feeling about what so engaged me as "subject." That is, I didn't necessarily begin writing a poem about something to discover what I felt about it, but rather I could find the articulation of emotions in the actual writing. I came to realize that which I was feeling in the actual discovery possible to me in the poem. So I don't choose my subjects with any consciousness whatsoever. I think once things have begun—that is, once there are three or four lines, then there begins to be a continuity of possibility that they engender which I probably do follow. And I can recognize, say, looking back at what I have written, that some concerns have been persistent, e.g., the terms of marriage, relations of men and women, senses of isolation, senses of place in the intimate measure. But I have never to my own knowledge begun with any sense of "subject."

In fact, I fall back on that sense of Olson's where—I think it's "Letter 15" in the *Maximus Poems* where it goes: "He sd, 'You go all around the subject.' And I sd, 'I didn't know it was a subject.' " You see, I don't know that poetry has "subjects" except as some sort of categorical reference which persons well distinct from the actual activity put upon poems for, I suppose, listing in library catalogs. Poetry has *themes,* which I feel are somewhat different; that is, persistent contents which occur in poetry willy-nilly with or without the recognition of the writer. These themes are such as I've spoken of, war and the others. But I don't feel that these "subjects" are really the primary evidence of the poem's merit or utility in the society in which it occurs.

Wagner: You don't, then, have any "point" to make, to use a common term of reference?

Creeley: I have a point to make when I begin writing insofar as I can write; that is, the point I wish to make is that I am writing. Writing to me is the primary articulation that's possible to me. So when I write, that's what I'm at work with, or that's what I'm trying to gain, an articulation of what confronts me, which I can't really realize or anticipate prior to the writing. I think I said—to egocentrically quote myself—in the introduction to *The Gold Diggers,* well over ten years ago, that if you say one thing it always will lead to more than you had thought to say. This has always been my experience.

Wagner: To look a little more closely at those themes, then. Many seem to deal with love, hate—in short, human relationships. Is this human interaction the dominant interest in your milieu, from an artistic point of view?

Creeley: Well, I've always been embarrassed for a so-called larger view. I've been given to write about that which has the most intimate presence for me, and I've always felt very, very edgy those few times when I have tried to gain a larger view. I've never felt right. I am given as a man to work with what is most intimate to me—these senses of relationship among people. I think, for myself at least, the world is most evident and most intense in those relationships. Therefore they are the materials of which my work is made.

Wagner: Then, in general, are you writing about what is personally most important to you?

Creeley: Yes. People are the most important things in the world for me. I don't at all mean that in a humanistic sense. I am a person. And how my world is, is intimately related with how all other worlds of persons can be. So that they are the most insistent and most demanding and most complex presence offered to me. I am never, never apart from that as a concern in working.

Wagner: In some ways, this kind of subject is different from that of many of Williams' poems, which you admittedly admire. Is there a contradiction here?

Creeley: Again, remember what Williams does say, "The poet thinks with his poem." So that when he has a poem such as "The Red Wheelbarrow," which it would be interesting to remember occurs in that sequence *Spring and All*, a mixture of poetry and prose in its original version. That poem, and that whole sequence, is a way of thinking in the world, a way of perceiving—not decided upon but met, that is, almost met in full course, by "divine accident," as Stendhal again says. So that there is a choice; choice does not exist except as recognition. Williams says that that sequence is moving among the recognitions that are given him of the perceptions he can offer. And what I am interested in in those poems is not the—not only, let's say—the literal material evident in the red wheelbarrow, but in how the perception occurs, how he thinks in the context of that relationship. Not simply why does he say this, but *how* he says it, how he gives it credence, how he gives it recognition. I've always been fascinated by this in his poetry—not so much how did he do it as how did he put that car together; to look at or feel or sense or hear, how this way of thinking occurs. I'm fascinated by the way people think and feel (thinking is feeling and feeling is thinking and so on). The materials of Williams' poems in a literal sense are not indifferent to me by any means, since they are the material of his world, which is very attractive to me—but I don't feel that it's a contradiction.

Either he or now as younger men, myself—we are both doing something quite akin: we're thinking, we're gaining an articulation for ourselves in the activity of the poem. As he says, "In our family we stammer until, half mad, we come to speech." That or "the words made solely of air" that he also mentions in these two poems from *Pictures from Breughel*. This context for poetry is one always very intimate and immediately recognizable to myself. So I don't think that you can say, "Well, this man talks about green bottles and this man talks about his wife; therefore, they are not interested in the same things." I don't think this is so simply to be said. It's the way these things are perceived in the poem and how they are articulated that is significant; and in that respect I would feel a great debt to Williams and would feel that I had learned much from him indeed.

Wagner: What is the modern poet to do, then, with Eliot's objective correlative? For instance, your poem "The Immoral Proposition" is successful, but it seems to have nothing one could relate to this particular term.

Creeley: The catch in that whole preoccupation is the literality that's intended and, unhappily, it isn't the kind of literalness that really is consistently useful in Williams' writing. The question is whether or not one will admit something like "I feel sick" as being a literal condition or a literal thing, let's say. Does feeling sick have a literal occasion? Or is it an abstraction. We'll say you feel sick because you haven't eaten anything or you have typhoid or are bored; you know, there are many contexts in which that statement could have meaning. So that what I would try to make clear here is that in a poem like "The Immoral Proposition," I am involved with the substance of an emotion, with a very distinct content of feeling—which I hope is evident in the poem. A way of feeling in some circumstance that I feel to be substantive. I don't obviously claim for it a like substantiveness as, say, what a block of wood proposes or a stone, but at the same time I feel that feeling is substantial and is literal and can be articulated; and I am working my way through its terms in that poem. Again, in a sense, I am feeling my way along as I am writing.

So that if it's abstract, it's abstract in quite a different way than, say, those statues of hope. I'm not trying to make emotion *less* substantial in the poem. I'm trying to articulate it and all that I can feel in it, as I confront it in the writing. I'm not trying to summarize it nor to conclude it nor to take it away from its active environment. I'm really trying to gain the experience of that environment as I am writing. So again you see, I would feel the very end of that poem offers the most succinct statement of what abstraction or this kind of egocentric possibility in itself does lead to: "The unsure / egoist is not / good for himself." That's a real condition. That's not abstract. I meant literally, that he's not good for himself in that he tends to be stuck in self-destroying conjecture: he worries all that he confronts to pieces because he is so unsure in his activity, and simply ends by defeating the possibilities of his own life.

But, no, *abstract* means removed from its condition, removed from its own term—to drag away, literally, as with a tractor. That kind of abstraction I've always felt a great uneasiness about; but when the situation of some thing, be it emotion or actual potato, is left to exist in its own intensity and in its own organization, then I don't feel an abstraction is involved. And *objective correlative,* by the way, as a literary term is a very unwieldy and awkward and very deceptive sense of things, I feel, because it tends to the context of symbolism. It proposes that the thing for which there is an objective correlative is in some way a symbol of that object. And I feel that *that* really is the disastrous mistake. There's nowhere else for things to be except where they are, and if this is realized, then much time indeed is saved. Words are things too. If I say "I love you" or "I hate you," each one of those words—I-love-you—is a thing. Words are things just as are all things—word, iron, apples—and therefore they have the possibility of their own existence.

Wagner: While we are discussing the subject matter of your poetry, let me ask about your most recent book, *The Island.* That's wrong, isn't it? *The Gold Diggers and Other Stories* would now be the most recent. Well, using both the stories and the novel, the prose seems to me very close to your poetry, not only in its careful, polished style, but in its themes. Do you feel that all your work to date is of a piece?

Creeley: Effectively so, by no means intentionally so, but insofar as anyone is this kind of thing we've been talking about— or does have this insistence of his own existence and his own organism and his own organization as such—just so all that issues from him is particular to himself. I don't mean style. I mean if it's the issue of him, then it will have a continuity, whether he intends it or not.

I remember years ago, again in a letter from Louis Zukofsky about one of the books I had sent him of my own—after talking about the various poems in it, he said, "Well, we write one poem all our lives." In other words, any one part of that poem may or may not have individual significance, but it all goes together as one continuing writing. To make divisions in it is a little specious because it does in that way necessarily cohere. I find, then, that I can't write outside of my own "givens." These are the things that I'm given to work with and I can try to escape them, but I never succeed in any interesting fashion. So that for me the novel is the continuing of writing that I've been trying to do now for almost—what?— twenty years. It doesn't take a place apart from the poems, nor is it different from the poems in its concerns. It's all an attempt to articulate some complex of feelings that are gained through the writing, that otherwise are not to be gained. I remember one time in conversation with Ramon Sender, he was saying, "Well, anyone, an eleven-year-old schoolboy can write a poem. The emotional equipment is there even that early. But," he said, "now think of the problem of gaining an articulation and an actual placing for each word in a novel— that's 50,000 to 75,000 to 100,000 words which one is responsible for, the conduct of each word."

Now a novelist that I respect does feel that way about what he is doing, and I certainly felt that way about this novel: I felt that each word had to have as much justification in its own position as, say, any word in a poem. I'm not here claiming that the novel is a poem because they are very different modes, but I felt that a novel was responsible to words in just the same way that a poem is responsible, and that the conduct of words in either situation had to be the responsibility of the writer in all possible senses. Not that he had to "justify" them by some explanation specious to their activity, but that they had to engage in an articulation that was significant to his own feeling. And that they had to find their place in the context in that way. Elsewise it was all a proposal of not very much interest at all.

Wagner: With all this personal feeling in a work, how can the writer avoid writing a "true confession" story? The age-old problem, how does he maintain the proper perspective, whatever that may be?

Creeley: There is no "proper perspective." Really, I can remember in writing classes in college, one professor would tell us, avoid all autobiographical reference because you will have such a subjective sense of it that you will not be able to approach it coolly or objectively.

Therefore you'll find yourself involved with distortions because of your writing about yourself. It will be disastrous, etc., etc. Then I'd go into another class and be told there that all one could really use was autobiographical material because that's all one really knew. All the rest was too removed from the intimacies or intensities of one's own experience. You see now, either of those adamant rules is a little specious.

One *knows* in writing, I don't know quite how, but one knows what one needs and one takes it, without embarrassment and increasingly with a demand that's not to be gainsaid. So that there's no reason why one shouldn't write a true confession story. Again I'm thinking of Stendhal who wrote a brilliant true confession story, *The Life of Henri Brulard*, and equally something like *Lucien Leuwen*. Or there's a quote to the effect of Stendhal saying apropos Julien Sorel, "Julien Sorel, c'est moi." Again, writing makes its own demands, its own articulations, and is its own activity—so that to say, "Why, he's simply telling us the story of his life," the very fact that he is telling of his life will be a decisive modification of what that life is. The life of the story will not so simply be the life of the man. The modifications occurring in the writing will be evident and will be significant.

I don't feel that a proper perspective is of any use except in cases where there is a clear need for it—that is, to keep your head while others all about you, etc., etc., à la Kipling. There are circumstances evidently where that kind of coolness or objectivity is much required. Or there are kinds of writing in which it is. But in writing it doesn't really matter whether one is literally out of one's head with the insistence of what's being said, with the emotional demand of it; or whether one is working at a cool and quiet and objective remove from what the material suggests as emotional possibility. Again, you see, Rousseau's *Confessions*—that to my mind is an extraordinary work. I'll never know Rousseau, any more than anyone else will, but that book is a great relief of feelings that are very much of the human context. Therefore their admission into the writing with such intensity and clarity is already a great relief of all that surrounds him. To read that book is to be relieved.

In other words, I've never felt that writing was fiction, that it was something made up about something. I've felt that it was direct evidence of the writer's engagement with his own feelings and with the possibilities that words offered him.

Wagner: The issue of "distance," then, is an invalid one?

Creeley: The distance is dictated by the poem, not by the writer. Or the assumptions he may bring to it. The writer may begin writing coolly about something about which he feels no possibility of involvement exists, though why he should want to write about such a thing I don't really know, but suppose he does so begin. To me, it's such a large absurdity; it would be like living with someone from whom one could maintain a discreet distance. What would be the point of that? Writing to me is the most intimate of all acts; why should I want to maintain a distance from that which engages me in it? True, there are times in writing when I want the sight of something, or when I want to gain the view of it that will rid it of my assumptions about it. But that distance, you see, is dictated by something very intimate in the writing. It's not to be proposed prior to the writing unless one is writing instructions for assembling washing machines. But, again, the circumstance will dictate that need much more ably than the writer can propose, and much more significantly.

Wagner: I've been interested in this matter of the difference between poetry and prose, Bob. Since you have been writing both for many years—with the short stories the earlier, of course—what do you find to be the major differences between the two modes?

Creeley: Well, let me again speak personally. The differences as they exist for me are these. Poetry seems to be written momently—that is, it occupies a moment of time. There is, curiously, no time in writing a poem. I seem to be given to work in some intense moment of whatever possibility, and if I manage to gain the articulation necessary *in* that moment, then happily there is the poem. Whereas in prose there's a coming and going. Much more of a gathering process that's evident in the writing. In fact, I think I began prose because it gave me a more extended opportunity to think in something—to think around and about and in terms of something which was on my mind. It hardly gave me this sense of objective distance we've just been talking about, but it gave me the possibility of stating the thing that occupied me in a variety of ways.

For example, an early story like "Three Fate Tales" would be an example of this. It's fairly clear what's on my mind there—how is one in the world—and these three takes on that sense of situation are really what the story consists of. Also, I was involved at the time I wrote the novel . . . well, I was very interested to gain the use of something that would go on, that would give me a kind of day-to-day possibility. Now in the actual writing I found that it occurred quite otherwise; that is, in some ways I was back to a circumstance which I had come to know in poems. And I must note here that stories were usually written the same way—in one sitting; so that I wasn't really aware of how much time they were taking until I'd finished and looked at the clock. Maybe two hours or four hours had gone by, and I'd been writing.

But those stories too had the same kind of context, and the same sense of demand in them that the poems came to have for me. I think that I was probably more articulate in prose than in poetry at first, in the early fifties, as the second issue of *Origin* will probably show. You can see from that kind of evidence that prose was much on my mind; I was more at home with its possibilities at that time than I was with poetry's. In any case, prose lets me tinker, rather than work in the adamant necessity of its demand upon me. I come and go from it. I can work at many levels of response and can articulate these many levels—whether intense or quite relaxed or even at times inattentive. Prose, as Williams says, can carry a weight of "ill-defined matter." Well, I don't know if it's necessarily ill-defined but it can be random, and even at times indecisive. It doesn't have to say everything, so to speak, in one intense moment.

Wagner: And poetry does.

Creeley: Usually. And also this sense of continuity, of having something there day after day was something I've had a great longing to have the use of. I had distinctly envied Olson the possibility of the *Maximus* poems—that they could provide, as Olson calls Pound's *Cantos*, a kind of "walker" for all that one could feel in writing—or by means of writing. Robert Duncan had had this also I'd felt in poems like "A Poem Beginning with a Line by Pindar" and very much in "The Venice Poem," which was the first poem of his that really seemed to me major. So I tried to write a novel earlier, when I was living in France in the early fifties, but there the program of the writing became so intrusive that the actual possibility of the writing leaked out—I was so intent upon how do you make a transition from one chapter to another that this is really all that survived in the writing. I did get from one chapter to another with some grace, but what the actual writing was doing was largely lax and ineffectual. I don't mean that it had to move mountains but it was really unengaged except by the technical concerns that I was then trying to work through.

Wagner: Any explanation for this state of affairs?

Creeley: Well, I didn't really have anything on my mind of much pressure, of much necessity. Whereas the stories of that same period—"The Grace" and "The Party"—were much more intensive and much more an issue, I would feel now, of things I was confronting in my life. Therefore I would feel they are much more pressured. They have the fact of reality and the pressure as I would always feel again those two things to be a necessity. I think that's a quote from Olson—or from myself. I can't remember which. So, talking then about the differences. Those are some of them. That is, for me personally poetry is an intense instant which is either gained or lost in the actual writing. Prose is much more coming and going, though my own habits in writing prose are very much like those I do have in writing poetry: I don't revise as a rule, I find it necessary to begin at the beginning, to go forward, so to speak. I remember again in conversation with Sender, he asked "Why don't you simply begin at some point that's of intense interest to you, to what you think to be dealing with?" I said, "Well, I can't really do it that way. I can only come to that. I can't anticipate it by going to it directly. I have to arrive at it, and I don't even—curiously—know what that point will be. I'll have to find it." Not at all to be sentimental, but I think again that writing for me is a process of discovery, and I mean that very literally: a way of finding things, a way of looking for things, a way of gaining recognition for them as they occur in the writing.

Prose offers me a more various way of approaching that kind of experience than does poetry, but then I do have the sense that Pound speaks of in *Make It New*, that one chafes if something in prose is of interest, to have it, frankly, in the articulation of poetry. Simply that poetry offers the finer and the more intense articulation. Now this isn't always true in the sense that there are moments in prose without question (in the writing of Stendhal again) which are as intense and as charged as any I've ever experienced. This is certainly true of Lawrence, and of Dostoevski, and of many prose writers indeed who have this ability to articulate a very intense emotional context; but the finer articulation is possible for me in poetry. With one exception, that I am embarrassed as yet to manage in poems the kind of coming and going that I've only been given to manage in prose.

Wagner: Of the two modes, which do you prefer?

Creeley: Well, again, I don't prefer either. I'm led to use either as I can.

Wagner: A matter of necessity, then?

Creeley: Yes. When poems offer—just that they come to be written, then I feel very akin to Williams in that sense he speaks of in "The Desert Music," apropos the question, "Why do you write a poem?" "Because it's there to be written." I've never really to my own knowledge had any other sense of why things are written. They simply come with such a presence that one does or doesn't manage it as one's own abilities can. But—I don't prefer it either in that way. I don't say poetry is more useful for me in this sense, and prose in that sense; and therefore I write a story when I want this effect, and a poem when I want that effect. They come and go.

When something's been on my mind for a long, long time

and I've been in some sense conscious of it, then very often it will be prose that gives me the possibility of articulating what is so dogging me with some emotional insistence. I've been thinking, for example, recently of a park in England where I was sitting with a friend, and I was very new; I felt not alien but freshly arrived, as I was. We were sitting in this quiet park on a Sunday afternoon, a small sort of intimate family park with walks, not hidden exactly but people moved along almost corridors of trees and plants so that one had a constantly changing vista of persons as they came and went. And then there was a kind of old statue, not particularly distinct or admirable but sort of interesting as a kind of old person that had suddenly been immobilized or concretized.

But in any case, that moment, sitting on that bench, talking in this rather random fashion and watching the people and seeing children all ages, is really on my mind. Now, you see, I don't know what I'm going to do with it—or rather, I don't know what it's going to do with me. But that kind of insistence—it's been in my mind, curiously; it's one of the most intense things which I seem to have gained in England. I don't know what it means. I don't understand it. I don't know why it should be—of all the kinds of experience that I had there—that moment suddenly is awfully intense. But you see at some moment that's probably something that's *coming* to be written. I feel it now, that it's coming, that I shall work with it. And when I do work with it, I would feel it will probably be with prose because it's such a shifting; it has such a complexity in it that I'll want to move with it tentatively. Prose allows me a tentativeness which I much enjoy at times because it's a need. That is, I don't want to anticipate the recognition of what's involved so that prose gives me a way of feeling my way through things. Whereas poetry again is more often a kind of absolute seizure, a demand that doesn't offer variations of this kind.

Wagner: You plan to do more prose, I assume, as well as poetry?

Creeley: Yes, I do plan to do more prose. I must say, though, that as soon as I *plan* to do more prose, I do absolutely nothing. I had planned to do another novel because I really enjoyed very much *The Island*; and so having learned in a sense some of the technical possibilities of such a form—that is, having written it—I gained some insight into what technically was possible in a long prose piece. I wanted not to lose it, so I very quickly committed myself to do another novel, which was unwise of me.

Once I had proposed to do the novel, even gave it a title, and had what I thought was a good occasion (those two years I had spent in Guatemala had given me a crazily chaotic impression of so many things and persons and acts—such a wild variability of people in such a very curiously primal place—that I thought, "This is an ideal thing to work with in prose"). But as soon as I plan to do it, I've all but stopped it. I don't know how I am going to get past that. One day I'll simply sit down and start writing. Until that day comes, talking about it is a little absurd because I simply don't work in that fashion. By planning, by planning to do the novel, and by talking about it with my publisher, accepting a small advance and giving it this title and all, I seem—well, one moment last spring, for example, I really got almost hysterical about this and called the publisher and said, "Look, I want to pay you back that money. I'm sick to death of the whole program of this writing." No, again, you see, Pound is so insistent in the basis of my own critical estimations of my own circumstance. That quote he has from Remy de Gourmont, "Freely to write what one chooses is the sole pleasure of a writer." That is so true. So that as soon as it becomes programmed in any way, in the sense that it isn't momently recognized, it's a very, very problematic context in which to try anything.

Wagner: Have you any plans for writing criticism?

Creeley: Criticism for me is occasional writing. I'd never undertake it as anything more. It's my own attempt to respond to something that's moved me, and to give witness to that response and to that which has provoked it. And to define the character of my own respect for something that's evident. At times I feel it's a very weak act on my part, that I've not really measured to that which has offered me measure, as with Zukofsky's work, for example. I feel a great ineptitude confronting it because it's been such a source for me and when I'm trying to write a review of it, I'm a little embarrassed to gain an articulation of all that concerns me in it. For example, I've committed myself to do a review of Robert Duncan's *Roots and Branches*, in 500 words—that will be like the ultimate telegram.

Again, I think of critical writing as primarily a response to the act of some piece of writing that really has been very, very important to my own perceptions, and very important in my own recognition. And I tend more and more to shy from critical writing as a kind of chore or as a way of reporting. For a time I was involved with writing omnibus reviews of books of poems, and this very soon got impossible. I found myself playing a kind of odd game of checkers where I would balance this against that; in other words, I was imposing upon these books a falsely comparative standard.

Wagner: Does the pursuit of prose of whatever kind make you any less a poet?

Creeley: Well, I'm not "pursuing" prose. I'm not after it. And I certainly don't think it . . . I would like to qualify the situation of myself as writer: that the modes are the particular possibility that's evident in the situation of the writing as it's being done. And I think that what I would say, if I had the guts or the lack of embarrassment, that I would say that I would rather be a "writer" than a "poet" or a "novelist." So that then I would use whatever mode was relevant to the things given me to write, as they determined it, not me. Ideally, one should be able to make use of any mode that gained the most insistent, fullest range of articulation.

Wagner: The use of any mode betters skills, then, of all?

Creeley: Words are the materials of writing, and all that sharpens one's sense of their possibility is useful. Therefore, either prose or poetry can improve skills in the writing of either. I think, for example, I learned a lot about how to continue by writing the novel, and it seems to me true that my poems show what's gained in that novel. "Anger" or "Distance" or "The Dream" or "The Woman"—all of these were written after the novel, and all demonstrate that there's a possibility of going on in the poem that hadn't been there previously. There are only a few poems of this order prior to the novel—one is "The Door," but its sequence is determined by an almost rhetorical term of argument. I had been depending upon a continuity that was taken pretty directly from the rhetorical terms of thesis, antithesis, etc. In other words I followed a habit of organization there that I don't think I was aware of. Much more interesting to me in its organization is a poem like "For Love," but that was curiously a one-time possibility. Since the writing of the novel, when I found how things could drift and shift, and how the line might encompass that possibility— because the line is an extraordinarily important part of the novel's articulation; that is, the way the sentence is going is very, very important. I don't mean simply to say that sentence and line are equivalent but they do offer something of like possibility in their own circumstances.

Anyhow, I'd learned things from the novel—how to approach, how to feel things—that were then useful to me in the poems. And I think poems like those I mentioned come pretty much from the experience. I remember Duncan saying that he felt that the rhythmic articulation in the novel had really gone beyond what the poems prior to it had accomplished. And I would feel him right.

But you see, I'm not interested in being a poet or a novelist as something that has a stable content. I don't think that being a prose writer makes one less of a poet because I don't think one is made—except in historical reference—a poet or a prose writer in that sense. I'm very much against the kinds of division that, for example, led to Lawrence's poetry being ignored for such a long period when his novels were so much appreciated. That kind of division is specious. If a man's a writer, very often one will find the same intensity of possibility in all that he does. Very often, say, a prose writer finds it difficult to move into the organizations of poetry because they are very, very articulate and if much attention isn't given them, they don't just fall simply to hand. It's a highly articulate craft which is accumulated with many hours and years of attention, but I find, for example, Pound's prose is just as interesting in many senses as is his poetry. The critical writing, not only in what it says but in the way it's written, is a very vivid and intense kind of prose. I've learned from it. I think, again, that some of Lawrence's poems are magnificent, and the kinds of intensity they possess are those familiar to me in his prose also. So I don't like these kinds of specious division that say a man is "either-or," and that no actual relation between the two circumstances can easily exist.

Wagner: In speaking of the methods the poet uses to reach his poem—the forms, rhythms, other devices—I am always curious about the actual writing itself. One hears so much about the conflict between a supporting occupation and writing. How long does the writing of a poem take for you?

Creeley: For me, it's literally the time it takes to type it— because I *do* work in this fashion of simply sitting down and writing, usually without any process of revision. So that if it goes—or, rather, comes—in an opening way, it continues until it closes, and that's usually when I stop. It's awfully hard for me to give a sense of actual time because, as I said earlier, I'm not sure of time in writing. Maybe to me it seems a moment and it could have been half an hour or a whole afternoon. And usually poems come in clusters of three—three to six or seven. More than one at a time. So that there will be a period in which I'm writing. I'll come into the room and sit and begin working simply because I feel like it. I'll start writing and fooling around, like they say, and something will start to cohere; I'll begin following it as it occurs. It may lead to its own conclusion or to its own entity. Then, very possibly because of the stimulus of that, something further will begin to come. That seems to be the way I do it. I have no idea how much time it takes to write a poem in the sense of how much time it takes to accumulate the possibilities of which the poem is the articulation, however.

Wagner: Your surroundings during the time both of accumulating and writing—how significant are they?

Creeley: Milieu—what each person will need for what he has to do, cannot be qualified simply. Allen, for example, can write poems anywhere—trains, planes, in any public place. He isn't the least self-conscious. In fact, he seems if anything to be stimulated by people around him and by moving in large situations of people. For myself, I need a very kind of secure quiet; not so much from the noises of the house—Beatle records in the next room, I could write with. I usually have some music playing, just because it gives me something, a kind of drone that I like, as relaxation. It helps me. I remember reading that Hart Crane wrote at times to records because he liked the stimulus and this pushed him to a kind of openness that he could use. In any case, the necessary environment is that which secures the artist in the way that lets him be *in* the world in a most fruitful manner. Some people love much company; some love very little. I tend to be a person who feels best in some kind of privacy. I have very close friends and happily a large number of them, but I don't find them easily met or easily gained in large clusters. I don't like large parties; I don't like to be confined only to literary people, because I do have a kind of uneasiness about the "rest of the world" and therefore I'm much reassured when I have friendships with men or women who are quite apart from the literary process or activity. I like a family. I'm very involved with domesticity as a fact or as a condition of living. But it's hard, again, it's awfully hard to make a general answer to such a question.

Wagner: What is your concept of the creative process *per se?* Would you agree with Williams' description of it? theoretic know-how plus "the imaginative quota, the unbridled madsound basis"?

Creeley: Yes. One can learn a lot both by reading and by what you've accumulated by writing yourself. And then it's up to— god knows quite what it is—it's up to these occasions that come without much announcement and declare themselves, as Williams says, because they're there to be written. All the understanding of process in the world to my mind doesn't ever guarantee their occurrence. And one curiously never does know just when or why or how or in what guise they will be present. In other words, the know-how gives one the further possibility of being able to follow what is so being declared. That takes all the accumulation of technical ability that one can muster. And it's awfully frustrating to feel the thing shifting and realize one doesn't have the competence to follow it. This is a very unsettling and irritating event. That's where the technical ability does make a difference.

Wagner: No one can learn to write poetry, then? This total involvement of the poet—experiences, knowledge, technique, emotions—one is a poet perhaps by virtue of what he is, not by what he knows?

Creeley: He's a poet in the sense that he's given the possibility of poetry by what seems to be a very mysterious process indeed. At the same time, all that he knows from his own writing and that of other writers helps to gain him as much articulation as he can manage with what is so given him to write. It's rather like driving. A man who can't drive at all is obviously embarrassed to go down a road that's opening before him. The most articulate driver is he who can follow that road with precisely the right response to each condition there before him. I would feel those might be in some way equivalent contexts.

Wagner: You speak a great deal about the poet's locale, his place, in your work, particularly in *The Island*, of course. Is this a geographic term, or are you thinking of an inner sense of being?

Creeley: I'm really speaking of my own sense of place so that I want to avoid "a" sense of "the" poet's locale. I mean many things. I mean something like where "the heart finds rest," as Duncan would say. I mean that place where one is open, where a sense of defensiveness or insecurity and all the other complexes of response to place can be finally dropped. Where one feels an intimate association both with the ground under one's feet and with all that inhabits the place as condition. Now that's obviously an idealization—or at least to hope for such a place may well be an idealization—but there are some places where one feels this more intensely possible than others.

I, for example, feel much more comfortable in a small town. I've always felt so, I think, because I grew up in one. I like the rhythms of seasons, and I like the rhythms of a kind of relation to ground that's evident in, say, farmers; and I like time's accumulations of persons. I loved aspects of Spain in that way, and I frankly have the same sense of where I now am living. I can look out the window up into a group of hills seven miles distant from where the Sandia Cave is located, the oldest evidence of human occupation of this hemisphere. I think it dates back to either 25,000 or 30,000 B.C. and it's still there. And I can think of this place as a place where men have been for all of that time.

And again I'm offered here a scale, with these mountains to our southeast, which we sit in the foothills of; with the Rio Grande coming through below us to the west; and then that wild range of mesa going off to the west further. This is a very basic place to live. The dimensions it offers to those who live here are of such size and of such curious eternity that they embarrass any humanistic assumption of men as being the totality of all that is significant in life. They offer a measure of persons that I find very relieving and much more securing to my nature than would be, let's say, the accumulations of men's intentions and exertions in New York. So, it is both a geographic term and the inner sense of being that's permitted by that term.

Wagner: Another aspect of locale, I think, is the association among poets. I realize you have just finished participating in the Berkeley Poetry Conference, with Allen Ginsberg, Charles Olson, Philip Whalen, and many others. Two years ago you took part in a similar session at the University of British Columbia. Evidently, you feel such meetings are useful?

Creeley: Well over thirty people read at the Berkeley Conference. Olson, Snyder, Duncan and myself taught seminars. Ed Dorn read and lectured; John Wieners read. It was a large number of people indeed, all primarily from the context defined by Don Allen's *New American Poetry.* It was a very exciting company. As to being useful, I don't know actually what the public effect is. There was a very large response to this one in Berkeley; a great many more people came to the readings than was expected. To see, for example, well over a thousand people giving Robert Duncan after his reading a standing ovation that lasted for at least ten minutes is to experience the possibility of a response to poetry that I didn't think I would ever live to witness.

I was talking also to Allen who had had the experience in Prague of one hundred thousand persons turning out for his having been crowned King of the May, which was not to give him a personal accolade but rather to regain this kind of presence among people in a very literal manner indeed. This festival has very archaic roots and this figure—that they had made Allen—was very significant.

But in any case, personally, I've become a little weary of public events. I think I need some privacy for a time, but I'm always stirred and moved and grateful for the company that these conferences do involve. Because I do live in an isolated sense, that is, away from many of the friends that I have in this way; and these are the few opportunities that I can get to be with them.

I do, however, suspect the universities' appropriation of these conferences. I think the universities begin to realize that the arts are enjoying a very insistent public approval these days. For example, at Buffalo—I was there also for the Buffalo Arts Festival—and was to be in a symposium with Randall Jarrell and an English poet named Hugo Manning. Just before the actual meeting these two men couldn't come and so W. D. Snodgrass and Robert Graves were got as substitutes for them. We walked into the auditorium where we found ourselves confronting a crowd of well over 2,000 people, who had come to hear a discussion of "Poetry Today." Equally, the first day of the Albright-Knox Gallery's opening of their kinetic art show, they had over 14,000 people. And I understand the Metropolitan Museum is widening its steps in order to permit the crowds that now come to it. Also, the number of persons visiting museums, primarily in New York for weekends, is larger than the attendance at baseball games in the same area.

But I question the universities' trying to make the arts a *subject*. And I always will question it. I would much rather feel that the university was reflecting a public concern with the arts rather than some institutional concern that wants to gain them as materials for its own activity. Till they realize that the arts are not to be confined by their assumptions, there will always be rancor and a feeling of misuse.

I came away from the University of California, for example, feeling in one sense misused indeed, because we were subject to a structure that was very uncomfortable and did not permit our free movement within it. Even such simple things as the fact that we were not given any help with housing, we were not given any parking space for our cars, we were told that it would cost $75 to purchase a parking permit for this two-week period because there was no other means offered. In other words, there was a curious indifference to ourselves as persons, having the very real problems of our families with us in several cases. At the same time we were, curiously, "stars." We were given great use in this way. The University of California at the time of my going out planned a publication of the seminar, which was happily dropped; and we were recorded endlessly and by people as far flung as a professor from the Sorbonne. National Educational TV was there to film on location and to interview us outside of that. But I do question the context if the arts are to be treated only as further subject matter for universities; if that's what they're after, they miss the point entirely.

Wagner: At one time, artists clustered in several cities. Now, however, there are many "isolatos"—Vassar Miller, Robert Bly, James Wright, yourself. Why?

Creeley: Unlike painting, for example, which does require some kind of location (if you want to see what's going on in painting you live in Los Angeles or New York, simply because the galleries and museums in those places are active reference), but you can send a book to somebody who lives five million miles away. Writing doesn't require that you be present. And after a certain age—I think when one's young it is extremely important to be in close contact with people that are stimulating in a way that you're all going through, trying to find what's particular to your own possibility—but by the age of 35 or 40, one is about one's own work in a more decisive and more determined fashion. Once that time happens, then it is not necessary to be so closely in touch with others. I, for example, like the isolation, or at least I find it useful to me. At times I balk against it very much. But I like it in that it gives me long uninterrupted periods when I can work, no matter what I may be doing for a living. I find I can pay attention to what's really confronting me more simply in this environment than I can in the city where I'm distracted by both curiosity and sympathy, by all that's going on around me. And it isn't so much that it won't be of use to me, but I mean, I can't—I've got my work to do just as these other men have their work to do, and in order to do it, I need a time and privacy that's particular to myself.

Wagner: Could we return to associations for a moment? You've mentioned Olson and Duncan and Ginsberg frequently. I know you are friends, but what influence has the writing of, say, Olson, had on your own poetry? Have any poets really been important in the development of your art?

Creeley: It's almost impossible to qualify that sufficiently. Olson was the first reader I had, the first man both sympathetic and articulate enough to give me a very clear sense of what the effect of my writing was, in a way that I could make use of it. His early reading of my stories particularly was very, very helpful to me. I found him the ideal reader, and have always found him so. At the same time, his early senses of how I might make the line intimate to my own habits of speaking— that is, the groupings and whatnot that I was obviously involved with—was of great release to me. I had been trying to write in the mode of Wallace Stevens and it just hadn't worked. The period, the rhythmic period that he was using, just wasn't intimate to my own ways of feeling and speaking. And so, much as I respected him, I couldn't use him at all. Williams came in too and he had large influence, but it was Olson curiously enough in the "Projective Verse" piece (I think I'm right in saying that the first section of that is taken in part at least from letters that Olson wrote me, the part about from the heart to the line, where he's explaining his sense of the line and the relation to breath). So he really made clear to me what the context of writing could be in a way that no other man had somehow ever quite managed.

Denise Levertov certainly in those early years was very important to me. We talked so much and exchanged so much sense of mutual concern while living in France. She's very important to me; we both share the respect for Williams and the interest in problems of writing. Paul Blackburn in the same period also. Robert Duncan is one of the most warm and sympathetic friends I've ever had, which is very important to me, and again is one of the most astute and involved readers I've ever had. And Allen equally, because Allen reassured me as Williams had that my emotions were not insignificant, that their articulation was really what I was given to be involved with. Ed Dorn—many, many men. It's impossible to list them all.

Wagner: Would you say that the influence of a poet's contemporaries is as strong as his "ancestors," so to speak?

Creeley: Very, very much so. I think as in the case of a university, very often students teach each other more actively than they are taught by their professors. Except that there will usually be one or two people of the so-called, "ancestor" type that are very important; Pound is very important in this way. Williams, although I felt him in a questionable way contemporary always; Whitman finally comes to have for me this possibility, although I must confess I'm beginning to know Whitman in a way that I hadn't known him previously. Hart Crane had this effect for me. Then the very precise beauty in Stendhal; for example, the way the thought was so free to find its own statement—and to only move as it was feeling some response. Then the peculiar beauty of, say, Wyatt or Campion. Shakespeare in this particular period was very, very moving to me. Coleridge, I used to love to read Coleridge in the diversity and the multiplicity of his statement, as I loved James for very like reasons. Or Jane Austen. In other words, I don't think one can make an absolute statement apropos which of these two possibilities is the more important. It depends. It depends simply on who one is and what one's particular nature leads him to.

Wagner: Do you credit any one writer with a strong influence on your poetry?

Creeley: I think Williams gave me the largest example. But equally I can't at all ignore, as I've said, Olson's very insistent influence upon me at that early time and continuingly. Nor can I ignore the fact that the first person who introduced me to writing as a craft, who even spoke of it as a craft, was Ezra Pound. I think it was my twentieth birthday that my brother-in-law took me down to Gordon Cairnie's bookstore in Cambridge and said, "What would you like? Would you like to get some books?" "Gosh, yes," and I bought *Make It New*, the Yale edition. That book was a revelation to me insofar as Pound there spoke of writing from the point of view of what writing itself was engaged with, not what it was "about." Not what symbolism or structure had led to, but how one might address oneself to the *act* of writing. And that was the most moving and deepest understanding I think I've ever gained. So that Pound was very important to my craft, no matter how much I may have subsequently embarrassed him by my own work. So many, many people.

I could equally say Charlie Parker—in his uses of silence, in his rhythmic structure. His music was influential at one point. So that I can't make a hierarchy of persons.

Wagner: There exists at the moment a large group of young poets writing what have been called by some, "Creeley poems," short, terse, poignant. Will these young writers stay imitative?

Creeley: No, they won't. Imitation is a way of gaining articulation. It is the way one learns, by having the intimate possibility of some master like Williams or Pound. Writing poems in those modes was a great instruction to me insofar as I began to "feel" what Williams was doing as well as "understand" it. And so I found possibility for my own acts.

I think therefore that this imitative phase is a natural thing in artists; and I would feel it should be encouraged. I think that if so-called writing classes would use this possibility, possibly they would produce a more interesting group of craftsmen than is now evident. This is one way to learn, and it's the way I would respect, coming as I do from a rural background where learning how to plow is both watching someone else do it and then taking the handle of the plow and seeing if you can imitate, literally, his way of doing it; therefore, gaining the use of it for yourself. But what you then plow—whether you plow or not—is your own business. And there are many ways to do it.

With Lewis MacAdams

I met Lewis MacAdams during his time as a graduate student in Buffalo. Both he and his close friend Duncan McNaughton had come from Princeton and now took Jack Clarke as their mentor. I was intrigued by them, bright, various, very contemporary as one says. McNaughton, brilliant, wry, often depressed in those days, was determined by the responsibilities of his marriage and wanted to do right by his exceptional wife, Genie, who in turn gave up her own academic commitments to foster his. There was never an easy way. Lewis, on the other hand, seemed destined for Andy Warhol glory, and he and Phoebe, his wife to be, reminded me of a comfortable glamour I'd only known edges of. Again that seems a bleakly simple gloss in retrospect.

Whatever, George Plimpton had given Lewis the job of adding to the material that Linda Wagner had accumulated, to loosen it up a bit, make me seem more humanly various. He was adept at it, as times since have much emphasized. I am thinking particularly of the documentary he subsequently made on Jack Kerouac as well as the extensive journalism he's managed in Los Angeles. He has also proved an ample and engaging poet, warm, specific in his judgements, alert to the common world.

His accommodating preface for Donald Allen's initial publication of all this interview in Contexts of Poetry *(1973; p. 51) makes an active sense of things as they then were:*

> *The first try at this interview was a failure. Creeley was ready, but I had just driven the New York Thruway from New York to Buffalo; and by the time I got to Eden I didn't have any questions left to ask. The "interview" ended in the dark, everybody morose and slightly drunk. So we adjourned to his driveway to shovel snow. We tried again two weeks later, in March of 1967. The snow had stopped, the sun was out, and*

71

the Creeley household was full of friends, the poets Allen Ginsberg, Robert Duncan and Robin Blaser; his wife Bobbie and their daughters, Kirsten, Sarah, and Kate. After breakfast Creeley and I went upstairs to his study, a big sunny room looking out across a long wooded valley to Lake Erie. The study had once been a nursery and the framed photographs of Charles Olson and John Wieners, and Bobbie were set off by a pink wallpaper covered with tiny horses and maids. On one of his bookshelves was a tiny piece of sculpture by John Chamberlain. The tape continues to roll . . .

MacAdams: Why is it in your works that New England rarely figures as a geographical place at all? It seems more like a language.

Creeley: As a kid, I used to be fascinated by people who, like they say, "traveled light." Perhaps this is the same kind of metaphor that the *things* my father left in the house after his death were too—I was very young and these *things* were really "my father," whom I never literally could remember very clearly otherwise. My mother even took care of them, or kept them, like his bag for example, or his surgical instruments, or his prescription pads, or, even to quite a late time his doctor's bag still had the various pills and what not in it. It used to be fascinating to take all these pills and see what they would do to you. The things were not only relics of his person; but, what was interesting to me, there was this instrumentation peculiarly contained in this thing that he could carry in his hand. The doctor's "bag," for example. I was thinking of the idiom now, "bag," to be in this or that "bag." That that doctor's bag was an absolutely explicit instance of something you carry with you and do your work in. As a kid, growing up effectually without a father, I was always interested in the particular people who entered our house as men, that I had particular feeling for as men, would be men who'd come to do something; like say, a carpenter. Or who came with specific instrumentation; e.g., tools. And what fascinated me as a kid was the idea that you could travel in the world—Johnny Appleseed, for example. Or images or senses of traveling in the world with what you needed in your own hands. That fascinated me.

And that does come back, for example, when I find myself talking to people apropos writing. One of the persistent scenes will be that it's first of all, say, "What a great thing. To be a writer." That words, you can carry in your head and they're free. You don't need any particular materials other than the most minimal. And that given anything, possibly, to write on; and even if you don't have something to write on, you can possibly induce your memory to retain it. That you can really "travel light." I had minimal involvement with the Depression, unlike Bobbie, but the sense of being able to travel with what you need was very fascinating to me. First of all, people would always be telling you you ought to carry in your head what you need to know. And that secondly, you ought to be able to move at a moment's notice; because the world was such that if you couldn't thus move, if you were hindered or impeded by some necessity to be where you were as though you could not move from it, that you'd miss the chance.

MacAdams: How old were you when you left Harvard to go into the American Field Service?

Creeley: Eighteen.

MacAdams: Did you just do one year at Harvard?

Creeley: They did accelerated programs during the war years, and I entered in the summer of 1943, and so when I left I believe I was in the middle of my sophomore year. I took a year off, effectually. And I was a copy boy, living in Cambridge, but working in Boston. But I was only that for three or four months. Then, I was suspended from Harvard. I carried a door out of Lowell House that the painters had removed to paint. An afternoon. So . . . Then I remember that was extraordinary, to get on a boat in Baltimore, and to get off the boat in Bombay, that was about 28 days at sea, and sailing through the Mediterranean so you could see Port Said, for example, but you couldn't get off the ship because of security.

MacAdams: Did it feel like total dislocation, or like great adventure?

Creeley: Great adventure. It was fascinating. It was a lovely time. I was sort of glad to get out of there. The whole scene around Cambridge was rapidly deteriorating. My job was getting incredibly tedious. The rapport with my first wife to be was increasingly meager. We were in love, but she had gone to Black Mountain College, and then she decided she didn't love me anymore, etc., etc., so that was all a very bleak occasion. And this really jumped me into something I had absolutely no anticipation of whatsoever. It was terrific. Grotesquely so, thinking of the occasion. But it was terrific.

MacAdams: Had you been in correspondence with Williams and Pound before that?

Creeley: No, no. That only came after I was out of college. We first went to Provincetown where we spent a year. We came to be there because I'd met a man who was very good to me, in the sense that he talked to me a lot, and he was outside the academic scene. He was a writer named Slater Brown. He was at that time at a kind of bleak period of his own life. He was working as a gardener in Belmont.

MacAdams: He's Cummings' friend, "B," in *The Enormous Room*, isn't he?

Creeley: Yes. He was a writer of the same period as Cummings. And I gather he was active on *The New Republic* for a time. And that he was also active on *Broom*. So he thus had acquaintance with Allen Tate and Malcolm Cowley, and he knew all that particular group of people. But his closest friend of that group would be Hart Crane. Slater and his wife were really about the only people of this relationship that Crane speaks of consistently with affection. When I first met Brown his own scene was pretty bleak. He'd been drinking heavily for a number of years. He was effectually an alcoholic. But he had these fascinating stories. And so we went down to Provincetown, which was a bohemian community, and we stayed there for a year. And then we decided, hopefully, to buy a house in New Hampshire. We had a friend who had a place he was interested to sell, which we began to buy. So we lived in New Hampshire for three years near Franconia Notch. It was during this time that I started writing to Pound and Williams apropos a magazine I was involved in. That's how I got up my courage to write them. I would have been shy of writing them just to say, "I think you're a great man," or something. You know, I wanted to have business that gave me reason. And that happily did. Pound wrote specifically, but he tended to write injunctions—"You do this. You do that. Read this. Read that."

MacAdams: Did you do everything he said?

Creeley: I tried to. I couldn't do it all. He would send books at times which would be useful. *The History of Money* by Del Mar, which I read, thought about, and so on. He was very helpful. It was very flattering, to be taken at all seriously by him. Williams was always much more specific. And at times would do things which would—not dismay me—but my own ego would be set back. I remember one time I wrote him a very stern letter—some description about something I was going to do, or this was the way things were blah blah. And he returned me the sheets of the letter and he had marked on the margin of particular sections, "Fine. Your style is tightening." But I had the sense to know that it was of more use to me than whether or not he approved of my answers. He would do things like that which were very good. While Pound would say, "Would you please tell me how old you are? You refer to having been involved in something for forty years. Are you 23, or 63?"

MacAdams: Who was the person to first hear Olson?

Creeley: Well, Olson had met Duncan when he had been out on the West Coast. I think in the late forties. He had been out there, and he had been introduced to Duncan, and he had had a very vivid impression of him. He said he went to a party, I guess, at Robert's place. And he found Robert sitting on a kind of velvet throne, looking like Hermes himself, or something. He was very amused and impressed by the incredible drama that Robert was able to make of the scene. And "Against Wisdom As Such" would be some of that. But I think Robert was so involved in his own scene then, or so involved with the center of writing he'd got to, that I don't think he had much interest in Olson at this point. Olson really comes into Robert's purview, so to speak, through *Origin*. But the first person, curiously, to give us access to Olson was Vincent Ferrini. He heard from Cid Corman that I was trying to get material for a magazine, and so Cid had asked Vincent to send some stuff, and then Vincent undertook to send some of Olson's. And my first reaction was that I wrote back saying, "You're looking for a language." And, boy, did he ever come back on me!

MacAdams: What did he say?

Creeley: He said, "Let's take that up. Am I looking for a language?" You know, "Am I looking for a language? In ways perhaps that you haven't considered." No, I didn't even know how old he was, frankly.

MacAdams: Were you in New York at this point?

Creeley: No, no. Still in New Hampshire. Then about a year later, it must have been, we moved to France. So that I really was writing to him for almost five years previous to meeting him. It was a very intensive correspondence, by which I mean sometimes four or five letters a week would be going back and forth.

MacAdams: Were you raising pigeons at this point in the country?

Creeley: We were in the process of buying this farm. As a kid I'd had poultry, and pigeons and chickens and what not. We had no ambitions that this would make us any income. We had a small garden that gave us produce for canning. And then the chickens did afford us eggs and meat, but they were never any real commercial scene. And we were living on a pretty small income, and it gave me something to do. It made the form of a day very active and interesting. I mean, something continuing: feed them, pluck them, take care of them in various ways. And I had met a lovely man, indeed, named Ira Grant, who was a house painter in Hanover. And he was also a crazy, decisive breeder of Barred Rocks. He was a lovely man. Quite small, almost elfin in various ways with this crazy, intense, and beautifully articulate imagination. He could *douse*, for example, and all manner of crazy, actually mystical businesses that he took as comfortably as you'd take an axe in hand. No dismay, or confusion at all. This happened several times with neighbors in New Hampshire, e.g., losing money in the woods. You'd just cut a birch wand, and find it. The same way you turn on the lights to see what you're doing. It can be variously hazel or birch, or hard wood, preferably, that grows near water. You can usually get it in the form of a forked stick, and when it dips, there you are. Continuingly, in parts of New Hampshire, if you wanted to find water, the most economical and simple manner of finding it would be to get somebody in the neighborhood that had this ability, and ask them to come over and check out various places for you. And they had good luck. I mean Ira would be almost always right. I remember one of these neighbors of ours, Howard Ainsworth, a woodcutter, was cutting pulp in the woods on a snowy day like. But he had a hole in his pocket, and by the time he had discovered it, it was late in the day, and he'd lost a pocketful of change. So Howard simply cut himself a birch stick and he found it. It was nearly total darkness in the woods and he found it. He only remarked upon it, that is, how he'd found it, as an explanation of how he'd found it. I mean, it never occurred to him that it was more extraordinary than that. "Wouldn't anybody," you know.

MacAdams: How did it strike you?

Creeley: I was fascinated by it. Because it was the kind of quote mysticism unquote that I could enter into, because it was so extraordinarily practical and unremoved from its actual location. Ira had this crazy way of exemplifying what he knew as experience of things. He used to paint, for example, you know paint pictures. He showed me once this picture of a dog. He said, "What do you think of this? It's one of my favorite dogs." He showed me this picture of a dog that looks—it's a picture about this large—not very big. And it's this white and black dog that stands there looking incredibly sick. And I said, "Gee, Ira, it's a nice picture. But." And he said, "Yes, it died three days later." He said, "That's why it looks so sick." But he delighted me, you know; and I felt much more at home with him than with the more—not sophisticated—because I don't think any man was more sophisticated in particular senses than he. But, God, he talked about things you could actually put your hand on. He would characterize patience or how to pay attention to something, or, you know, how to have not so much continued occasion as though one wanted it; but how to pay attention to what's happening. So in a funny way he probably gave me more sense of things than almost any man I can think of. I have some of his letters still. He wrote in a lovely old-fashioned hand. A very warm man. Extremely good to us. I think he sensed that we as a young couple were really having a bad time, very confused with ourselves, and very unable to admit our own condition. And he curiously managed to permit us to do that.

MacAdams: You were open to it?

Creeley: I sure was. I was very anxious to, not so much to know what was wrong, but to know what was this continuous state of frustration. He never really told me, but he permitted me to see it.

MacAdams: How come you went to Mallorca?

Creeley: The situation with the house we were trying to buy was getting very tight. In other words, we fell through on one payment, as it happened. And the owner decided that since we'd failed to pay this particular business, we should either pay it or get out. So we decided that we couldn't really keep this scene together. It was just too expensive. The house was awful. It was a lovely house but it was in complete disrepair. We spent an awful lot of money, such as we had, trying to get it back into shape. I mean the roof was gone, the floors were gone, the sills were gone, the whole place was overgrown with brush that we had to clear. There were many things that needed repair. We put in a heating plant. But he got very—I don't know—I think he just decided it was interesting to have his house back. I don't think it was some kind of great economic scene, but I think he now became interested in the place. Simply that we had sort of broken the ice. So we were trying to live on, it was literally $215 a month. So we decided that living on that amount of money in New Hampshire was really bleak. People were getting sick. Everything was very expensive, or at least it was more expensive than that amount of money could provide for. Mitch and Denise [Levertov] Goodman had gone to France, and we wrote and asked them what kind of a life was possible on that income, and they said, "Fine, you can probably live very well." So we went over and we ended in a house. Whoo, awful house we had, although I got to love it. But it had no lights, no water, no heat, no electricity, no toilet, no nothing. It had a little wood stove— this business of crawling around in the winter out in the woods adjacent to this little block of houses that sat out in the farm country away from everything, trying to knock down dead trees and cut 'em up with a marine knife to burn in the stove. It was really weird.

MacAdams: Do you think you work better in that kind of isolated position?

Creeley: My habit seems to be so still, although having been now a teacher for some years I can make it with a number of people and find a place with a number of people. But my dilemma, so to speak, as a younger man, was that I always came on too strong to people casually met. I remember one time, well, several times this has been known to me, I tended to go for broke with particular people. Once I found access to someone I really was attracted to—not only sexually, but in the way they were—I just wanted to—I found myself absorbing their way of speaking. I just wanted to get in them, literally, to be, to be utterly with them. And some people, understandably, would feel this was pretty damned exhausting to have someone thus hanging, you know, like coming at you. And also, I didn't have any experience of how it was really affecting the other person. I mean, I think that a lot of my first wife's understandable bitterness about our relationship was the intensity that she was having to deal with. I mean everything was so intense and thus was involved always with tension, and that my way to experience emotion was to tighten it up as much as possible, and not even wittingly. Just "naturally." One time I remember, I was with someone, Dan Rice, who's an old friend from Black Mountain, and he and I were in some situation with other people and we were talking with someone we'd just met, and I remember when the other person either had gone to the john or something, Dan just sort of said, "Look," you know, "like, don't come on so strong. It isn't that you're arguing or anything, but the intensity with which you're forcing this person to react or to admit you is really getting a little scary to them." See, I was always trying to push the particular circumstance to where it would break open, and be quote itself unquote or manifest itself; and understandably there are, I mean people in usual, like they say, casual daily activity don't really like to get, as they say, that involved. And I found my whole appetite was to be as involved as possible.

MacAdams: With everybody or just—

Creeley: Literally anyone met I wanted immediately to get into that condition. There are many kinds of explanation one could think of, psychologically and otherwise. You know a kid growing up with a peculiarly absent emotional condition except that there was a woman named Theresa Turner who continued to live with us after my father's death. She'd been almost literally rescued by him from a state home for the mentally retarded. She'd come to this country from Ireland as a young woman about eighteen or so to join her older sister;

and on entering the country she was given some kind of quali-
fying business that was customary and the immigration offi-
cials decided that she was not of a mental level that would
permit her to—so they referred her to this home for some
reason and he'd found her there, and he was a doctor, consult-
ing doctor for this home in Massachusetts. And he thus got
her out of there and she thus became a member of our family
and worked as a maid or whatever. She was so devoted to him
that when he died she continued to stay with us as a, effectu-
ally a housekeeper. But she was really the emotional center of
my life as a kid. Until she died when I was in my twenties after
I'd married. By then she had left our household and was
living again with her sister and her sister's family. But other
than her—I don't know how many people one needs—but
her inarticulation was very attractive to me at times—at times
it frustrated me awfully when I was in my early teens. The fact
that Theresa couldn't "get" some things that I could, say, was
very, very frustrating to me. But she really gave me an emo-
tional response, that my mother gave me too, but in a much
quieter more unintentionally reserved manner. And she was
also committed to making a living for us so that she was dis-
tracted. But anyhow . . . No, I loved to get with people, but I
didn't have any sense as to how you do it. I mean I was curi-
ously lost. My father being dead, I didn't know what the forms
were. How did you be a man? You know, immediately I
thought, "Gee, am I really going to be, not stuck with, but is it
my life to sit with the girls?" And I thought, "Well, I certainly
feel at home with the girls. And I dig their emotional condi-
tion because it's been my life." Growing up with five women in
the house, man, I knew all the signs and gestures and con-
tents, or at least I knew a lot of them that were manifest in
women's conduct. Ways of saying things, ways of reacting,
making the world daily. But I didn't have a clue as to what
men did, except literally I was a man. It's like growing up in
the forest attended by wolves or something. It took me a
curiously long time to come into man's estate. The sexual
initiation curiously doesn't resolve what people at times think
it does. I mean, they assume that when you've had sexual
experience somehow you are matured by it. I don't feel that's

true, necessarily, at all. Anymore than initial sexual experience at the age of ten or eleven, I mean your first experience of your body as this bag, that this necessarily has with it, that now today you are a man. So that for me to get to be a man was extremely awkward at times, and I learned it from my contemporaries and from one or two older men who somehow sensed my dilemma and were able to make forms that would give me articulation or show me how articulation might be possible.

So anyhow, I came on too strong, apropos living in isolation. See, I grew up in the woods. I grew up on a farm in West Acton, Massachusetts, that was not being used as a farm. My father bought it prior to his death and it was to be a kind of place for us to live while he kept his practice or business in Boston, or Watertown, Massachusetts. I could go out into those woods and feel completely open. I mean, all the kinds of dilemma that I would feel sometimes would be resolved by going out into the woods, and equally that immanence, that spill of life all around like the spring in New England where you get that crazy water, the trickles of water every place, the moisture, the shyness, and the particularity of things like bluejays—I remember taming barn rats. I mean, I was fascinated by animals and had early the thought to be a veterinarian, and actually by the time I was ready to go to college I had a scholarship to Amherst and to the University of Pennsylvania for pre-veterinarian medicine. I then shifted to writing. Or wanted to write, and so went to Harvard. Well, people delight me, but again it's that damned dilemma of wanting it all and not knowing yet—I don't think yet in my life I quite know how to do it. I like teaching, simply that teaching gives me a formal structure that permits me an intensive relation with other people. But otherwise in my habits I tend to, to need a space around me that lets me go to bed now and then. I mean, Allen Ginsberg makes a lovely remark that when I get to town nobody sleeps till I'm gone. I can't let anybody sleep because I don't want to miss anything. I want it all, and so I tend at times understandably to exhaust my friends—keep pushing, pushing, pushing. Not like social pushing to make a big noise; but you know, I don't want to miss it. I love it. I so love the intensity of people that I can't let anything stop until it's literally exhaustion. And immediately, in relations with the girls I then knew and loved. Again I'd want to push it right to the end. I mean, it wasn't simply fucking them. I wanted it all.

MacAdams: I've heard a lot of stories about your fighting in those earlier days.

Creeley: That's when the confusions of how to be with people became so frustrating and so unavoidable that I would just spill. And also I think it had a lot to do with drinking, which I did a lot of in those days. We were smoking pot, as we called it, we were smoking pot pretty continuously by about 194–. Let's see. I first had use of marijuana in India, where I was in the American Field Service. We were a barracks at one point of about 40 men. We had all ages and whatnot, and I think almost everyone in that barracks was turned on almost all day long. We were in central India. There was literally nothing to do. It was an incredibly awkward climate for us. I mean it was very hot and so we'd be sitting there sweating, and drinking was impossible. We drank as long as we could, until it was a question of vomiting half the day in this heat, and getting very damned sick. I had a friend from Southern California who one day suggested to me that there was an alternative. After literally bile for the last two hours coming out of your guts, he said, "Try this." There was nothing mystical. It was very, like, "Here, have an aspirin." So we switched and everything became very delightful. The food was instantly palatable and life became much more interesting. So that I remember, for example, returning from England on the *Queen Elizabeth*, being used as a troop ship returning Canadian troops back to Canada and the few Americans that were attached to British troops. And this friend and myself, we were both smoking a lot of pot on ship. In fact we used to get into the toilet. About 15 or 20 people would be depending on this toilet, and he and I would get in there and turn on, then sort of sit around. There'd be this great mass of people standing and waiting, banging to get in there. They thought we were homosexuals. This was aided by the fact that one night, I remember, I staggered into the room, and you'd have these tiers of bunks, and trying to get into my bunk, I climbed into the wrong one. But we used to get up on the boat deck, which was restricted, but we were there anyhow. So it was absolutely silent and isolate, seeing that whole sea in a beautiful full moon. Just beautiful.

Well see, had I had the sense, or rather had the situation been possible, I do feel that I would have relieved much of my life had I not been drinking in the frustration of social ineptness. And even to this day if I drink—I mean up to a point it's extremely pleasant and relieving and relaxing for me. But there comes an inevitable point where my whole feeling turns into irritation, frustration, and that's when I fight. I mean, I don't think I ever fought anyone except in that condition. I used to fight in just sheer frustration, and a feeling of absolute incompetence and inability. And also people were very belligerent during the forties and fifties. We used to get into these ridiculous fights. Happily I never got more than hit a few times.

MacAdams: I heard you had a fight with Jackson Pollock once.

Creeley: Oh yeah, a great meeting. Because he obviously was having, you know, intensively the same problem, with a vengeance. I'd been in the Cedars Bar talking with Franz Kline, and another friend of Kline's and Fielding Dawson probably was there. We were sitting over at a corner booth, and were talking and drinking in a kind of relaxed manner. But I, again, you know—very characteristic of me—I'd get all keyed up with the conversation and I'd start to run, get the beer, or whatever we were drinking, wasn't coming fast enough, so I'd, you know, I'd go back to the bar, have a quick drink, and return to the table and pick up the drink that now had come, and I was getting awfully lushed, and excited, and listening, so I was literally at the bar getting another drink, when the door swings open and in comes this very, you know, very solid man, this very particular man, again, with this intensity. So he comes up to the bar, and almost momently made some gesture that bugged me. Something like even where he put the glass on the bar, that kind of business where he was pushing me just by being there, and I was trying to reassert my place. So the next thing we knew we were swinging at each other. And I remember this guy John, one of the owners, just put his hand on the bar and vaulted, literally, right over the bar, so he's right between us, and said like, "Okay, you guys," and he started pushing at both of us, whereupon, without even thinking, we both zeroed in on him, and he said, like, "Come on now, cut it out." Then he said, "Do you guys know each other?" And so then he introduced us, and I was—God! It was Jackson Pollock! So I was showing pictures of my children and he was saying "I'm their godfather." Instantly affable, you know. We were instantly very friendly. And he was very good to me.

No, in those days, I remember, in the Cedars, I had a big wooden handled clasp knife, that in moments of frustration and rage—I mean I never stuck anybody with it, but it was, like I'd get that knife, you know, and I don't think I tried to scare people with it, but it was like, when all else failed, that knife was . . . not simply in the sense I was going to kill somebody, like a gun, but I loved that knife. You could carve things with it, make things and so on. And so, I'd apparently been flourishing it in the bar at some point, and I remember he took it away from me, John did, and he kept it and said, you know, like, "You're not going to have this knife for two weeks." And then he finally said, "Look, you can't come in here any more," and I said, like, "What am I going to do? Where am I going to go?" So he would finally admit me if I drank ginger ale only. Because I used to stand out front and look in the window. And then he would let me come in and sit, as long as I was a good boy and drank only ginger ale. And finally he let me have the knife back, because that knife was very, very—I've still got one like it.

MacAdams: When did you start writing about art? I never saw anything before that Frank Stella piece in *The Lugano Review.*

Creeley: Well, through Pound's agency I'd come to know René Laubiès, who translated some of Pound's *Cantos* into French—

the first published translation of them into French. And Laubiès was an active and interesting painter. In fact, I saw the first Jackson Pollock I ever really saw, in Paris at this friend's gallery, Paul Fachetti's gallery.

MacAdams: When was this?

Creeley: This must have been 1952. No, 1953. Up to then my relationships had been primarily with other writers. But I liked Laubiès extremely. It wasn't really the painting as something done that interested me. It was the painter, or the activity of painting I was really intrigued by. And so, at the beginning of that time I began to look at things. And then, because I was an American living in Europe, I was particularly intrigued by the Americanism of certain painters, like Pollock, obviously. And then I did have other friends, like Ashley Bryan, a friend of that time who was a painter. And so gradually I began to come into the relationship to painters that does become decisive. John Altoon, really, is the one who becomes very important to me because his energies were so incredibly—you know, the things he drew, made manifest in his work, were images in my own reality, so to speak. And then Guston was extremely good to me. I mean, was very good to me in the sense that he was very generous with his interest and time. I was fascinated by the condition of life these guys had. Not simply that they were drinking all the time, but they were loners and they were, they were peculiarly American, specifically American in ways that writing, except for Williams and Olson and Duncan—I mean, they had almost you might say the iconography of the peculiar American fact. And their ways of experiencing activity, energy—that whole process, like Pollock's "When I am in my painting"—that the whole condition of their way of moving and acting and being in this activity was so manifestly the thing we were trying to get to with Olson's "Projective Verse," the open field, you know, *The Opening of the Field*. And this was so much their fact, and Duncan actually in his "Notes on *Maximus*" makes very clear the relation to the painting that he'd felt in San Francisco with the group there—Clyfford Still and Diebenkorn and the whole roster of people he had as friends. That, curiously, was far more fresh as imagination of possibility than what was the case in writing, where everything was still argued with traditional or inherited attitudes and forms. So in the middle fifties anyhow, the painters, without any question, became very decisive for me personally.

I was thinking of when I saw John Ashbery two days ago. We were talking with editors and publishers, and at one point Ashbery gave his own sense of the New York School and its occasion. He said, "Well, first of all, the very thing it is, the one thing that we were all in agreement with, is that there should be no program, and that the poem, as we imagined it, should be the possibility of everything we have as experience. There should be no limit of a programmatic order." And then he went on to qualify his sense of the occasion, and why painters were to them interesting. Simply that the articulation—range of possibility—in painting was more viable to his sense of things than was the condition in writing. And I thought, "You know, that's literally what I would say. That's precisely the imagination of the activity I had."

Now we were caught in various geographical and habitual senses and thus for a time separated. You know, simply that we were intensely involved with the way we were feeling the articulations. But at this point, I mean we are all of us now roughly in our early forties, and what's striking is that each one of us of this nature has precisely the same grid of initial experience and proposal. And that we were finding that statement, I think, or that experience of it most articulately in the activity of painters in that period—late forties to the early fifties. John was obviously coming to it by way of the French surrealists or the writers of that kind. That's where he found, not only playfulness, but a very active admission of the world as it's felt and confronted, or met with. I was finding it in jazz, for example. And that's why Charlie Parker and Miles Davis and Thelonious Monk and those people were extraordinarily interesting to me. Simply that they seemed to have only the nature of the activity as limit. That is, possibly they couldn't change water into stone. But then again, maybe they could. That's what was intriguing.

MacAdams: Well, when did you start writing about painters?

Creeley: At Black Mountain I wrote a note apropos Laubiès, which I think is the first note of that order I wrote. Then, through the association with Black Mountain, I became very intrigued by Guston and by the visual, what's seen in the world and how all that can be complex. Because I'd been so involved with the economy of words as experience of sound and rhythm that suddenly it was like having things open again as things seen.

And so I wasn't in any manner of speaking knowledgeable as to what this scene was as some continuity historically. Nor could I use the vocabulary of the usual art critic. But I could, in Olson's sense, give testament, bear witness to this. My notes were of that order. I thought, I'm not arguing my experience of something as an ego proposal. But all I want to do is to say this has been seen in the world and this is my experience of it. Not as argument, but as invitation to come. You can see the relevance. We were making things. Not only of our own imagination, which was after all finally the point, but we were making things in the materials particular to our own experience of things, just as John Chamberlain was experiencing the particular fact of materials in his world, e.g., those car parts, and seeing how the imagination might articulate that experience; I was trying to make do with the vocabulary in terms of experience in my world. And neither one of us had history. Neither one of us had articulate experience of history, as something we'd come through as persons the issue of.

I remember Duncan, a lovely moment when we first met— he and Jess and Harry Jacobus had come to Mallorca. I was in a rather dense and difficult time in my marriage. Ann was away for some reason, that is, was down in the city shopping. We lived in a little house outside of the city. You got there by a trolley and the four of us were going back into the city to find them a pension that they could stay in. We were standing in this trolley with all the people banging around us. I remember Robert—we were all standing holding onto the straps and he looked—turned to me at one point and says, "You're not interested in history, are you?" You know, and I kept saying, "Well, gee, I ought to be. And I want to be. But I guess I'm not. You know, I'd *like* to be but, no, that's probably true." That history, as this form of experience, is truly not something I've been able to be articulate with, nor finally engaged by. So that art is, somehow, as Williams might say, the fact of something, but I did not have that alternative experience of it as an issue of time.

MacAdams: Do you think that comes out of Pound?

Creeley: Yeah; I think Olson says Pound, by virtue of the brilliance of his ego and that proposition that there are men in time that he can outtalk, or find as company for his own intelligence. And that there are, Olson suggests, only two that can possibly beat him at it: namely, Dante and Confucius. But that is still an issue of historical experience. And by the time I think I came alive in the world it wasn't a place like that. Although I am a person, let's say, of the generation that grows up in the Depression and then the Second World War, I wasn't located in it. By which I mean my mother had a civil service job. We were living in a marginal manner. I remember her salary in those years was about $2,700 to $3,000. And that was adequate in those years, I mean, it provided a stable economy. But we were sort of in that curious faintness of being neither in the world as some daily struggle with it, nor were we in any other world. We lived in a curious limbo and so there was nothing to locate us historically. How we'd all come to be in that house in West Acton was a kind of wild absurdity. My father had gone there with one imagination of it and my mother, for example, had grown up in Maine. They were very distinctly differing families. My mother's family were poor relations. Her mother had been an Everett. And because of the charm of this young woman, when young, her Boston relatives, or Cambridge relatives, had arranged for her to go West with Wendell Phillips on one of his missionary-like tours. And so she'd met Mark Twain, for example. They got as far as St. Louis, I think, and there was a young man in the company that she was supposedly to be interested by. But in the meantime she was in love with my grandfather who was the oldest of six sons from a French-Canadian Nova Scotia family. He'd gone to sea at the age of twelve, after his father died, to help support his brothers and his mother. And he was the antithesis of this Cambridge experience. So she went back after and married him anyway, and my mother, then, and her family would be the issue of that fact. And my father, on the other hand, was the only surviving child of this Scotch-Irish farmer who was in the Massachusetts Legislature finally, because he happened to live on Belmont Hill on a very desirable piece of real estate. So that as he stopped farming, he then sold his farm to the interests of that time and became quite wealthy, and seems to have enjoyed a very happy sort of senility—walked around Harvard Square in his bathrobe and slippers. Gave all his money to the housekeeper, obviously solace to him in his age.

I was the youngest son, my father had been married twice previously—I have two half brothers whom I honestly don't know at all. One of them changed his name in irritation and disagreement with my father's fact, and the other never married and lives in Chicago. So that there was a kind of blightedness one felt in their lives. But these were two older brothers that I never had really anything to do with. So I didn't know where the hell anything was. My father had died in this way. Then other echoes of the family were out there but never located.

MacAdams: Were your short stories written usually in one movement like the poems?

Creeley: Right, and again that's why I say that the kind of economy that Pollock was speaking of was very real to me. That is, when he said, "When I am in my paintings . . . ," that way of experiencing what he was doing was very known to me, and that equally, I remember one time in the fifties a conversation with Guston and my first wife. She'd challenged him apropos: "If you're painting this way, abstract expressionism or whatever you call it, how do you know when it's done?" She really was proposing that he was in some way a phony, and that this whole activity was in some way phony. And he took the question seriously, and gave her a very careful and generous statement of his own experience of painting. His resolution to this question as to how do you know when it's done was to say when you are thus both looking at and involved with this thing that's happening, and you can't see any place where further activity is permitted, then you're done. I mean, where everything has happened, what else is there to do? And I knew again that that was precisely how I felt writing, that when I couldn't say anything more, that was the end. Not I, again as ego, but when there was no more to be said, more accurately, that was it. And I knew that you thus continued writing and/or speaking until no further possibility of speaking was there. That was really the quote end unquote. Not that you got to some point of resolution that you imagined possible, but rather that you came to the *end* of it. And I thought this was what the particular men as Kline, or as Guston, or as de Kooning—not de Kooning so much because his formal procedure was rather different—but Pollock did. Absolutely. That they were not so much experimenting, but they were both delighted and moved and engaged by an activity that permitted them an experience of something, and that they therefore were with it as long as it was possible to be. And at some point it ended. I mean *it* stopped, and they were thus pushed out, or made to stop too, and that was it.

MacAdams: Didn't that come to be a problem when you wrote *The Island*?

Creeley: Yes. I'd previously tried to write a novel which I'd gotten so involved in as some technical circumstance—I mean I was so involved as to how you get from one chapter to the next, or one segment to the next, that all the writing became the articulation of devices, to have something go on or continue—to move from A to B. And the actual narrative per se is extremely dull. I wrote about 90 pages, actually. I threw it away finally. I was delighted that it all went together. But I was bored by what it said. So that, the most awkward thing I felt that I had to get past was, "How does something go on?" I mean, that is, "How does something start somewhere?" which, frankly, I feel might well be anywhere. And *then* continue. I mean, what agencies for that possibility exist? The poems I'd been writing, and the stories, had all been intense seizures or absolutely centered, you know, facts of emotional possibility, and involvement. And as soon as they exhausted their particular locus, or particular center in that way, they were done. That was the end of them. It was like a seizure, or a fit. But now one wanted to have something go on. I was intrigued obviously, by Olson's *Maximus,* and I was certainly intrigued by Allen's *Howl* and *Kaddish.* And I was intrigued by Duncan's "A Poem Beginning with a Line by Pindar." By that kind of possibility in Pound and Williams in *Paterson* and *The Cantos.* I wanted something that could go on. I was intrigued by Olson's reference to *The Cantos* as "a walker"—something you could take a walk with daily, and have as experience of daily possibility. And I know there was enough emotional center in that circumstance of the first marriage, but I didn't want to talk about it as though I had the decision of it. I didn't simply want to tell what happened. I wanted something I could now enter into, in 1960 I guess it must have been, that I could begin with. And I knew that the emotional confusion still hanging in the experience of it was enough. If I began speaking in this experience of something, I knew it would have enough energy to make something happen. But I was terrified. I said, "God, you know a novel is maybe 200 pages. On page one how can you imagine the possibility of page 200?" And it was Bobbie actually who said "Don't." I mean simply begin with what is, and then see how it is extensible or how it permits something to continue. This too, I got from Allen—Allen's sense that mind is shapely. That you don't have to think about thinking in writing in that way. You permit the experience of thinking to manifest its own condition. Bobbie said, "Simply start writing. Not start as some order. But begin with what is, and then see what happens. I mean don't worry about page 200. Don't worry about its being a novel. Don't worry about what kind of plot it can have. Don't worry about anything of that order. Just begin with what seems a particular possibility and write outward. Write from there." And it worked. Then I did give myself sort of hand-holds. Not in any sense of subject, but rather in the economy of the procedure. I know, for example, a story for me was five pages. This both satisfied me that there was enough of it. And that equally I felt that five page balance gave me a locus that was very useful.

MacAdams: What about the size of the paper?

Creeley: That changed. I mean at times the page would be bigger. Living in Spain I used legal-size sheets so that that would change the length of the stories. It wasn't a formula. It was just a habit—in the same way that, say the choice of paper and pencil or pen or typewriter were. It was part of the instrumentality. Just so, that sense of a five page context. It would be like buying a particular size of canvas. I felt very at home with that size of canvas, so to speak. I wanted to work in an economy of statement that had to do with a range of five pages. If you look at the manuscript you'll find that the chapters are all about five pages. The next question was, "How shall these be distributed, these five page pieces?" Then I thought, "Well, in fours." Four is a number that actually feels very comfortable to me, and yet has a variety of possibility within its own nature. Like one and three, or two and two. Or simply four. So that I can feel that that makes a viable balance. And so I then designed the circumstance as five chapters to each part. There are four parts. Four main parts. And then each chapter is in an economy of five pages in length, with five chapters to each of the four parts. And five times four is twenty, which is the number of chapters in the book. Which is sort of back to two again. I thought this was sort of—not cavalier—I remember trying to explain this to people, who would say, "Well, how did you do it? What did you have in mind for the plot?" And I said, "Well, you know, four times five." And they thought I was a nut or something. But, I remember one time talking to Douglas Woolf. I said I was using fives and fours. He said, "Do you know that last novel I wrote?" I think he was speaking of *Wall to Wall.* He said, "That's written in an economy of three, two, one." But it's written in that term of duration.

The problem is that in speaking of writing, usually if one says something like that, the literary critic, so to speak, is completely confused. Because he thinks of the organization of writing as having to do with symbolization, or with the development of character, or with plot. But he forgets that what's most interesting in that circumstance is what I would call the numbers of it—the phasing and the balances that have to do with number condition. Not with any assumption—I mean, hell, the novel isn't so much *about* life. Either it's manifestation of the possibilities of life, either it's life itself, or else it's something that I certainly don't want to carry like baggage along with me. So that phasing, just as it may occur in filmmaking, where it's equally a case, that is you can get a phasing of the relation of images in a one-two, or one-two-three pattern that really has much to do with how that enters, then, into the experience of seeing it, and in the case of a novel, of reading it. That four times five is an experience of not so much only a quote order unquote, but equally, I think, right back to that sense of the scale of the particular axis. Things like that. Those paintings of Pollock's which are distributed along the horizontal, as opposed to those which are vertical. That just so, in numerical balance, you have a curious and insistent initial experience of how things are going to come together. Anyhow, that was a great piece of information to have in hand when I was writing. I don't think I knew it consciously, but it felt good. It felt very appropriate. And it permitted me use of previous experience. That is, the stories. So that, instead of thinking of writing the novel, I thought of writing a sequence of such takes. Then I began to experience, as they continued, their interworking. I remember finally getting to the end of the book, and I'd literally written it in four weeks. I wrote in an intensive manner. By which I mean the book was written effectively. Although those four weeks occur in a two year period. When it was all done, I remember sitting down and reading through the whole thing, and just, I mean literally being gassed that it had all this interweaving that I had in no wise intended. I hadn't intended it. I hadn't thought of it. But in the writing it, it was part of the economy of writing it.

My only argument with people who think things previous to experience is that that becomes an awkward prohibition of what can happen in the actual activity. Again painters are relevant insofar as painters will tell you momently that to paint what you know, as Kline would say, is a bore to oneself. To paint what someone else knows is a bore to them, so one paints what one doesn't know. And the point of that is, the painting becomes a process of realization. Not simply an habitual insistence that this which we had known anyhow is still the case. Like "Yeah, Mother's still there. Father's still there. The house is still there." This is very boring information. At least in writing, for me, it's the kind of information that I, at times, deeply and truly depend upon. But in writing I want to be free. I want to range in the world as I can imagine the world, and as I can find possibility in the world. Of course we are within limits, as Olson would say, but it's to find where those limits are specific that's interesting. Pound, by the way, has a lovely note apropos Henry James' "pushing his limits in order to realize what they are." That is, he points to certain instances of James' writing where one feels, with hindsight, that the particular nature of James has been distorted in James' intent. That he's tried to do something which is peculiarly unsuitable. But how does one know, as Pound says, until one thus pushes limits to experience where they actually are occurring.

So that novel was great. That novel opened up a great deal of possibility for me. I remember Duncan saying, after he'd read it, "This really changes the whole formal occasion for you. Both rhythmically, and in the order of statement you previously had." And I think he's right. I think it permits poems like "The Finger" to be written.

MacAdams: Do you think it took this many years to actually occur?

Creeley: Yeah. I'd come to be in that time previous rather like a man who has decided that one thing is the case in all application. That there is one way to write. Or one way permitted to him to write. Short intensive poems. Short intensive stories.

MacAdams: Didn't "The Door" explode that at all?

Creeley: "The Door" was something that anticipated the explosion, let's say, but didn't realize it. I mean it realized it in its own fact of being a poem of this kind, but it didn't give me a continuity. The poem wasn't so much not characteristic, although I would then have thought so; but it came from experience I was extremely tentative with. I know the lady, as it literally says. But this way of moving around with a reality was something I hadn't previously been able to do. Let's say that there are impulses to this longer, or more various way of experiencing things. There are indications that this is hopefully going to be the case. That is, I was thinking of poems like "The Rose." Or poems like the final poem of that book, "For Love." But both those poems are rather recapitulations of previous experience. Although they get to terms of that experience that are being realized as the poem is written. "For Love" is really a kind of statement of "Look, we've lived in our lives in this way, and we have had this experience of them." It's the kind of note one would like hopefully to write to one's wife, or someone thus sharing life with us, saying "This is our life," like Williams' "Perpetual Mobile—The City." What's interesting about "The Door" is that it's moving into new occasions of experience, and by the time, hopefully, I get to writing, like "Anger," I mean that's not the rehashing of previous circumstance. That's an opening mode. And honestly, by the time I get to "The Finger" now, now the information is transformed. In the writing, and in the experience that the writing is getting to.

And that's what was happening in that damn novel. Because, hell, I knew what my life with this particular woman had been. I mean, we'd come to a divorce. I was separated from my children. I mean, if someone asked me, "What happened to you, Bob?" I'd say, you know, it was a mess. But in writing all that assumption of what had happened began to be transformed. And I began, not so much only to know myself, but John became a character, like they say. Not merely myself as some historical fact of something, but John became an experience that was new to me. I didn't know who the hell John was. And suddenly, John became someone not merely quote Robert Creeley, but rather became this wild viable extension of some imagination of someone by him or her self. Really, by the time I got to that novel I had a wild experience of how you think the world. That this man gave—John, I mean. He's not me as some kind of photograph of a previous reality or identity. He's now in the world as much as I am. People objected that the woman, Joan, is not given substantiality. Again, they're arguing a previous attitude toward prose as though a novel were to be fair to all of its people. And give everybody a chance. And the fact of the book is that it's the experience of thinking as creative reality; and hell, in that reality Joan had no substantiality. In fact, the very quote point unquote of the book is that this way of being in the world ultimately makes unreal all else that is in the world. It's like a cellular system in Burroughs' sense expanding to the point where it subsumes and distorts all other events, I mean literally, it tries to imagine—it's like that old business of God. Trying to imagine not only that God is, but that one is God. As though all creation would now be the fact of thinking.

A few weeks ago in Vancouver I had a reading, and I was trying not nicely or sweetly to make known to this young group the *horrors* of thinking that thought itself can possess the world. And I read that last chapter of *The Island*. I really was wanting to insist that this is what you can do to yourself, man, if you think *that's* an interesting trip. And that's why I kept writing "I want to get out of my mind." I mean, I didn't want a deracination of the senses, but wanted to get out of that awful assumption that thinking is the world. I was thinking how things have shifted, literally, in my experience of the world from that time of the forties when mind was thought of as the primary agent of having place in the world. I think that came probably from that sense of getting out of the whole nightmare of the Depression by being able to think your way out. And isn't that characteristic of Roosevelt's administration that there enters into American government in political circumstance a sense of expertise—the ability to think your way out of dilemmas; that is, to deal with the national economy by thinking of a way out. I mean, even the Second World War was a mind game. You confront one agency—isn't Hitler, for example, thinking the world is one thing; and then there are those obviously involved thinking it another.

But it honestly, to my mind, isn't until the sixties that people begin to, as Allen Ginsberg would say, come back into the experience of their own bodies as primary, and to realize that the mind is physiological. It is not some abstract deity that can be apart from the physiological moment of existence. I was thinking of that sense of Williams' of the interest in the mind and body as one. I think that if we want a center for experience now, it is this sense, that the mind and body are one. This to me seems one aspect of the revolution, in terms of human experience of itself, that is the human experience of him or her self in the world. It seems to me that we have moved from that duality that absolutely informs all my thinking as when I'm a kid, for example, that, you know, "the mind is to discipline the body," or "the body is to relax the mind." "You get drunk in order to relax your thinking. You think in order not to get drunk." It's a weird tension and the torque that's created by that systematization of experience is just awful. Just incredible. It can *whip*. You know I called a book *The Whip*. And that's why, that's why the title. I don't think I consciously went and said, "What's a word for this particular kind of experience, but that—I know—I wasn't to my own knowledge a sadist or a masochist. I knew that something whipped me constantly in my own experience of things. Something was really, you know, WHAM, WHAM, slashing and cutting me. And yet if I walked down the street I knew that nobody was coming at me in that fashion, so where in the name of heaven was all this taking place? Well, it was taking place in my thinking. Someone would hand me something pleasant, possibly, of whatever nature, and my momentary way of experiencing that was to imagine all that it couldn't be. Why am I being given this? What's the trick? Well, thinking asks "What's the trick?" That doesn't mean we have to be thoughtless. Or, it would take extraordinary discipline to be thoughtless, as Gary Snyder would testify. But it's very interesting that all of the people of my generation, so to speak, have each one of them come to some resolution of this dilemma with all the energy and all the particularity of thinking that they can bring to it. When Allen speaks of his ability presently to have a good LSD trip, what he's also saying is that he has finally been able to relax, not only to relax, but to get beyond the thinking that was the bad trip all the time. Or that when Gary is drawn to Zen, it's again to exhaust the mind's exercise of its will upon the body's nature.

MacAdams: When you tripped did you have any problem with that?

Creeley: I had momently one, when I entered upon the seriality of language. I remember at one point I did enter the dualism which is yes-no, that binary factor. I felt that momently it was going to be absolutely awful. I had just said something such as "this is the case" and I suddenly had an intensive experience of "this is the case—this is not the case—this is the case . . ." and then the identity of myself and all persons. It was not an ego loss, but it became—it was like seeing a vast checkerboard—that kind of alternating situation. Then I just, by grace of something, stepped out of it. Just stepped out. Then in the second experience with it, last summer, that blessedly never entered. And all through that second LSD experience I had Donovan's "There is a mountain." And I had equally a pleasant younger friend, and we'd taken it about two in the morning. We had a fire burning, and we were in an idyllic place in New England, at least in this way—fresh, and the woods. A beautiful morning. It would have been hopefully, anyhow, but I mean it was beautiful. The day broke clear and fresh and dewy, and there was all this moisture in the trees and the grass—those spider webs of moisture, and it was just idyllic. And the whole tone of the house became apparent in it. The children were without any consciousness of what we were in. They had obviously neither concern nor interest nor knowledge that we were on LSD, like they say. But somehow the whole information of this feeling went through the whole house, so that the girls had walked down to a store maybe a mile away and bought us a chocolate cake, which they gave us at one point. And they also spent about an hour and a half that morning making a necklace of pine cones which they gave Bobbie. The cats and our dog were, you know, almost ravenous for us. The cats were crawling all over us. It wasn't just our hallucinating and thinking they were. They were with us every moment—intensively, rubbing up against us and purring. From the fire in the fireplace that light, beautiful light, then seeing the dawn come up back of us as the room began to transform into the . . . So that "The Finger" is directly, you know, that information.

Now in this form. I remember that business of, and this woman—this beautiful primordial experience of woman, in the guise of my wife; but equally her image floating between the moments of birth—as girl-child as they say, to the most cronelike, the most haggish. Just crazily—all the guises of woman. All that Graves, for example, in rather didactic fashion tries to say is the case. I mean, he's right, certainly he's right. But it's not a hierarchy. It's an absolute manifestation throughout all realms of existence in this woman figure, and yet that woman is woman. She's unequivocally woman. It was absolutely delightful. I thus "jiggled the world before her made of my mind" and I thought, "That's the delight. That's what's meant when people say morphology, or men make form—man is form and woman is essence." Of course. But the pleasure is how the world comes to that point, and the delight is—that's like the dancing in the delight of thought, not the agony of thought as fixed pattern. But it's the delight of thought as a possibility of forms. When you get lost in those forms, for Christ's sake—when anybody proposes that those forms are necessarily correct or the only forms, *then* it's a nightmare.

With Michael André

We moved to Bolinas, California in the early fall of 1970, a much needed shift from our increasing dilemmas of habit. Nothing finally changed, but the completely transforming beauty of this edge of the west coast with its bluffs looking out to the Pacific was a beginning if any could be. The town had gathered an exceptional number of poets, Joanne Kyger, Tom Clark, Aram Saroyan, Bill Berkson, Clark Coolidge, David Meltzer, and Phil Whalen, among many others. And music was the base for it all, from the Jefferson Airplane to the fledging Rowan Brothers. Then Steve Swallow, jazz bassist extraordinary, lived just up the road and anchoring friend and painter from Mallorca days, Arthur Okamura, was always a shelter from the storm. I don't think I've ever lived in a more intimate and approving community than was the Bolinas of that moment.

So Michael André, fellow poet and editor, coming to interview me the summer of 1971, arrived in good season. With quirky humor and useful confidence he located me very aptly in my own concerns. He was apparently working to finish his graduate degree at Columbia (?) but far more to the point was his active magazine, Unmuzzled Ox, *which he had just begun to publish. I think one of the high water marks of the time was the special issue,* The Poet's Encyclopaedia *(Unmuzzled Ox 4, No. 4/5 [1979]), to which I contributed the definition of "stubble." I also wrote a "canto" à la Pound when he asked me to, and, later, veritable songs. He always read what I wrote with the kind of rapport one can only get from those working the same street. Clearly he knew and knows the right questions.*

André: Do you consider *Pieces*, your most recent book, an open poem like the *Cantos* or *Maximus* or *Paterson?*

Creeley: I'd had great respect for what Olson and Duncan had got hold of, let's say, with in Olson's case the *Maximus Poems* and in Robert's the whole sequence of *Passages*. It gave them a range and a possible density of statement that was very attractive. As a younger writer I had been most able to work in a small focus in a very intensive kind of address, so that I depended on some kind of intense emotional nexus that let me gain this concentration. But literally, as my life continued and I continued to live it, I really had a hunger for something that would give me a far more various emotional state, that is, the ability to enter it. And also I wanted a mode that could include, say, what people understandably might feel are instances of trivia; that is, I really respect Duncan's sense that there is a place for everything in the poem in the same sense that Williams says—"the total province of the poem is the world"—something of that order in *Paterson* somewhere—the sense that poetry isn't a discretion, that it is ultimately the realization of an entire world. So that I felt the kind of writing I'd been doing, though I frankly respected it, was nevertheless partial to a limited emotional agency and therefore I wanted to find means to include a far more various kind of statement through senses of writing I got from Olson and Duncan. Equally from Ginsberg who could lift, you know, some apparent instance of a very insignificant order into a statement—not verify or enlarge it but simply find a place for it. *Pieces* really became a kind of open writing in the sense that it was composed in a journal as daily writing. Sometimes weeks would go by, obviously, and nothing would be written. But the point is there was no need to have every poem titled, there was no need to draw a distinct formal line around every poem as though it were some box containing a formal statement: I simply let the writing continue almost as a journal might. And when the time came to publish it, I simply used the chronological sequence of its writing and let, say, three dots indicate that that was the end of a day's accumulation, and the single dots most usually indicate divisions in the writing as it's happening, as I was sitting down to do it. In other words, I wanted to trust writing, I was so damned tired of trusting my own opinion as to whether or not this was a good piece of poetry or a bad piece of poetry. That kind of dilemma really faded for me during the fifties and sixties. In the forties it had been a large argument:—what is a poem? By the age of forty or forty-five I thought if I don't know, it's obviously too late to learn. So I simply want to write in my own pleasure and forget that kind of signification that formal criticism insists on.

André: You've mentioned in your prose writing at various times that you don't have a "larger view," but that this is all right. Do you think perhaps this form, which implies an acceptance of "process," is a larger view?

Creeley: In some ways it is a larger view. I don't think it solves everything—simply that one's life goes on and the diverse conditions of it at various points of biological age begin to give information themselves—I'm now forty-five and I've lived in various relationships and various, you know, literal physical places in the world and it's impossible for me to feel that there aren't those literal changes in my own person. My nature seems to stay fairly anchored but a larger view accumulates as well as finds itself in some attitude towards the world. I thought the world was very large when I was eighteen, I thought it was so large I could never find a way in it. Then at times I thought obviously I can't live in the whole world so I'll simply stake out a place and hang on. That's about as absurd as planting a flag on the moon. If you've got that far you've got a lot further than you think.

André: Pieces doesn't have any national political discussions as do the larger poems of Lowell and Denise Levertov. Why?

Creeley: Why? Simply, the information of political attitude and/or conduct hasn't yielded me materials that I can make use of as a writer. I feel that writing is primarily the experience of language, and the diversity of contexts, and the diversity of changes and significations. I'm frankly and selfishly interested in the word. I'm interested in discovering what words can say. One dilemma for me in the political context has been the insistent didacticism of attitude, the locked mind that enters almost immediately with any political statement, the insistent rhetoric which places the words in an extraordinarily locked condition. Particular writers, such as Olson or Ginsberg or Levertov or Duncan or Bly, find it possible to use this condition of feeling as material, and to discover a language that can be this material. Myself, I haven't been able to do that. I've done a lot—not a lot—I've put my own commitments on the line, I think, by holding draft cards and by reading for the Resistance and I've had no intention not to state myself politically, but this hasn't entered my poetry. It's almost as if I've given so damn much to that idiot war I'm damned if I'm going to give it my experience of words.

André: One of your volumes of poetry was called *Words* and one noticeable trait of your poetry is that words which seem to have a common signification after a while take on an irreducibly puzzling air, for example, the word "form."

Creeley: Yeah.

André: It's used in so many different contexts; would you care to give a definition of one of these words?

Creeley: No—no, I wouldn't. "Form" has such a diversity of contexts possible to its proposal that it really depends I think on the occasion in which the word is finding place or is being given a place. I remember a lovely statement Wallace Stevens made years ago in reference to writing: "there are those who think of form as if it were a derivative of plastic shape." There are indeed a lot of writers who think of form as something you give the poem, that you take and shape it the same way you might shape a piece of wood to form a boat or whatever. I question that. Imposition of form upon words is always a problem for me—I've known men brilliantly to do it—Zukofsky, for instance, at one point in *"A"* gives a brilliant use of this kind. But form for me is something that's found in activity.

André: In *Pieces* . . .

Creeley: One last note on it. The only definition of form that really stuck in my head for years is really an instance, an example which I think is one of the very few interesting definitions of anything. It's a lovely quote that an old friend named Slater Brown once gave me. He said it was a definition from Blake though I've not ever found it [It comes from *The French Revolution* and is a characterization of the mob! R. C.] It simply goes "Fire delights in its form." That to me is the context I'm involved with.

André: In *Pieces* you have incredibly brief sections—I can't think of one offhand—which are almost concrete . . .

Creeley:

—it

it—

for example.

André: Yeah.

Creeley: Right.

André: Very brief poems.

Creeley: Right.

André: What do you think of concrete poetry, do you think it's arbitrary form?

Creeley: No. I think it involves what language has had as a visual context. The world has had the experience of seeing words for three or four hundred years as public events like billboards, posters, broadsides, whatever. It's not at all untowards to think that a poetry could evolve that was interested in words as a visual, as opposed to an oral, state of experience. And the poets I've known most interested in that are Aram Saroyan, a brilliant poet of this order—of any order for that matter—and Ian Hamilton Finlay. In both cases I think they have done extraordinary things with this possibility. As for example Aram Saroyan's very short poem—

eyeye

It gives a lovely reification of the eye, of the eye's activity, of the *two* eyes' activity. I think it's part of the possibility of language.

André: Similar to what you do with words, in the sense of stripping them of their commonness, you also take situations . . .

Creeley: I try to find their commonness—I don't want to interrupt you so argumentatively.

André: That's okay.

Creeley: I'm really trying to discover their common essence wherein they relate in an extensive way. For example, a friend here, Tom Clark, recently did a lovely book which is simply lines or quotations from Neil Young's songs and they compose an extraordinary book. I was also talking rather sadly in that sense to a friend here, Kitaj, who had used quotations from Zukofsky's poetry in a print that he did in honor of Zukofsky's poetry and Louis was upset that the words occurred without proper acknowledgment; there was a proper acknowledgment because the print made clear that this was a homage to Zukofsky. At the same time Kitaj, because of his own habits as a painter, hadn't thought to write for copyright, etc., etc., so Louis was irritated and questioned the use of the words blah blah blah. A person like Tom Clark would think, "who owns words?" Words are common. If you go swimming, you don't say: this is my drop of water and that's your drop of water. Obviously you're swimming in a common ocean. I really respect these young writers like Tom or Lewis MacAdams or John Giorno who don't worry about quoting in that awful sense. Everybody in my generation was involved with being original, scared to death they would sound like somebody else. Some of these younger men can sound like anyone in the world and I think it's delightful. Tom Clark, be it said, gives me the most accurate criticism of *Pieces* specifically in a poem called "A Sailor's Life" three or four issues ago in the *Paris Review*. That's criticism in Pound's sense of the use of the occasion that the initial poem springs from. And I have been very interested to see that that book's criticism has really consisted of people who know how to use the formal modes got to there. Not people who thought they understood what it meant. But the people who could demonstrate by their use of it that they were with its contents.

André: In your poems particularly prior to *Pieces* you tend to suppress the circumstances surrounding the poems, you tend to make your poems into general dramatic statements.

Creeley: Right.

André: Is that because you disapprove of personal life in poetry?

Creeley: No, the writing I've done at times has been felt to be so exclusively personal that people questioned its relevance to others. Even the landscape where the events were occurring was not that actively present. They didn't have a clue to its occasion except that obviously I felt it. One old friend felt that *The Island,* for example, was a private apology for a state of feeling, a relationship, and therefore questioned its use to other people. But I know what you mean. I wanted to strip away as much addenda as possible, to get it down to the nitty-gritty of the particular circumstance of feeling. I didn't want to argue that, o.k., that was true in Mallorca, but what would it be like in Boston? Or, of course it was true at four o'clock in the afternoon, but what if it were eight o'clock in the afternoon? I was trying to get not merely a "universal" occasion but I was also trying to strip away all that kind of qualification. I say "I heard" and you say "Well, you heard, what about me hearing?" You know, that kind of argument.

And then again moving into writing like that in *Pieces* and really beginning with information in *The Island* involved a continuity of statement that was really very new to me at the time. *The Island* was my first "long poem"; it was the first piece of serial writing that went on for many days, weeks, and so forth. It taught me a lot; it made me impatient with other forms of writing for quite a while. *Words* is an attempt to think of various other ways to move: towards the end those very short poems as in *Pieces* (in fact, "A Piece") begin to signal at least in hindsight what the writing was trying to get to, that is, a far freer context of statement. I really felt that if an elephant were not standing on your foot or if all your children hadn't momently died in some awful fire, then you really had no right to say anything.

André: There was a debate in the *New York Times* a few months ago between Richard Howard and Allen Ginsberg.

Creeley: I heard about it. Unhappily I didn't read it—oh—happily I didn't read it.

André: I was wondering who you'd side with in the debate, or if you'd side?

Creeley: Ginsberg. Well . . . yeah, sure. Wasn't it questioning the circumstances of the National Book Award?

André: Yes. Howard was upholding a "poetry of excellence," so to speak.

Creeley: I think a "poetry of excellence" takes care of itself. If one's at a time when world consciousness seems to be shifting in its dispositions towards experience, I think it's time indeed to acknowledge the resources of a far more extensive modality of statement than I feel Richard Howard does, despite what he gets to in *Alone with America.* In very real response to his ability, he's written perhaps the only essay on Gregory Corso's work that shows an active perception of Gregory's abilities. I think that's to be commended, but he is a critic.

André: Some people feel hostile to Howard.

Creeley: He's a strong man. He's got a very articulate head and he works. Most people feel hostile to people actively working.

André: You wrote a beautiful poem on Allen Ginsberg in *Words.*

Creeley: I've been deeply moved by his compassion for other human beings and his commitment to being with other human beings in the world. Characteristic of Allen, he's been recently at hearings here in the city, a federal commission on drugs, particularly on marijuana, and apparently he's cut his hair and he's wearing a blue suit and a felt hat, beard and mustache all gone, and when a *Times* reporter asked him what he was doing, he said he was "in drag." Which the *Times* misreported as "he said his previous state of dress was a drag." Speaking of politics, Allen is very alert. It isn't just that he wants to change his image but when his image becomes so habitual an appearance for other human beings, he's no longer interested in it—not if he wants to be active politically.

André: Your poetry has a kind of hip/beat air to it like Ginsberg; you deal with hallucinations and drugs and things like that.

Creeley: I saw a comment in a recent anthology to the effect that I was some sort of hip Emily Dickinson. Lovely thing. I thought she was pretty hip to begin with. I've been fascinated by diverse states of feeling, be it sitting in the sunlight or smoking marijuana; but I've certainly not used drugs in any conscientious manner.

André: Sometimes I know you're describing a state of feeling but I can't quite gather, practically speaking, what is going on. For example, there's a story, "The Dress," in which a man continuously imagines a cavern into which he will bring his wife and her friend. What brings him to this powerful kind of . . . ?

Creeley: I don't know. There's a cave across the street in that hill and at times kids come in here to borrow matches so they can go in the cave and look around. Now that's a literal cave back of a hardware store across the street and that cave is a very explicit experience: obviously to leap upon that as though it involved necessarily some symbolism—one symbolism for boys and another symbolism for girls—this might be some awful estimation of where they were in the cave. But that cave has a fascination for them. And if you live in a way that makes you uneasy in the so-called mundane world, think of all the imaginations of enclosure, the retreat some place where you can be sane, secure, you know, the whole business of wanting to get back to the womb, blah blah blah. Caves have a very initial sense of security. I was writing the story not in a sense of symbols, although obviously symbols are there, but in a sort of—surrealist would be my own estimation of that story's context. I wanted to state in surrealist terms the particular isolation I was feeling in the intensity of these two women's talking. My place became the imagined cave under the floor, and when I took them into it, I took them into the intensity and privacy of my own experience, with its own containment. Then I was using caves I knew in Mallorca. They have these wild stalagmites and stalactites which, you know, are obviously insistent sexual presences. So that the whole vocabulary sort of melted in this story which was really about the dilemma of the relation to a literal wife and her own senses of insecurity and the reassurance happily this other friend was giving her; and the dilemma of the dress and "who was she?" It's always fascinated me, that sense of the dress as becoming to you.

André: How Creeleyesque.

Creeley: I did not say it, it's what it said.

André: You recently seem to have gotten to another *state* of feeling—I don't know—in "Numbers," some of those little contemplations of a number seem mystical. Would you describe them so?

Creeley: That poem was written on the suggestion of a friend, Robert Indiana. He at first asked if he might use a selection of poems that were published to accompany this sequence of prints, of numbers from one to zero. I thought, wow, what would be far more interesting from my point of view would be to try to write a sequence of poems involved with experiences of numbers. In some halfhearted sense I looked up texts on numbers and got some information that way but it was immediately so scholastic and scholarly in tone that I couldn't use it I was really using something as simple as "what do you think of when you think of the number eight; is that a pleasant number for you?" I was thinking of sayings like "two's company, three's a crowd." I was thinking of the groupings implied or the imbalances implied or the odd numbers, the even numbers. Then other writing, like the last part of the zero sequence called "The Fool," is simply a quote from a text by Arthur Waite called *A Pictorial Key to the Tarot.* I just looked at that because to me it was a beautiful estimation of the experience of nothing.

André: One of the other poems in *Pieces* is titled "Canada" and it's only four lines long.

Creeley: It's a quote.

André: It's a quote?

Creeley: Heard on the radio, I believe. The CBC, no less. We were listening late at night in Buffalo and suddenly we were tapped into the history of the national emblem, etc., etc., and just those kind of grand proposals gave me the poem. I just like the way it went together.

André: Irving Layton was connected with Black Mountain?

Creeley: Really he was basically connected with Cid Corman and myself and Olson as part of the *Origin* group; an issue of *Origin* is devoted in part to Irving's work. And we in turn were contributing frequently to a Canadian magazine called *Con-*

tact, which was mimeographed and put out by Ray Souster and Irving and Louis Dudek. And that coincidence, that would have been in the early fifties, that coincidence of acquaintance and interest was really strong. I published a book of Irving's called *In the Midst of My Fever* and I published another book for him called *The Blue Propeller.* I was really involved by Irving's work; I thought it had a lovely, beautifully sensual lyric quality and I liked him indeed. That was before he was the "national poet."

André: In the first issue of *Black Mountain Review* there was to me very interesting attacks on Dylan Thomas and Theodore Roethke. Do you still stand by those attacks?

Creeley: Yes. In fact, again Duncan and I were talking only yesterday about the situation of another young friend, and why it is something is persistently unclear in his work. As Duncan put it, he hasn't yet come to his person, his person is not given him in poetry. There are those writers who really feel the primary activity they're involved in is getting something said, e.g., "there are eggs in the icebox" or "it's raining outside" and they are interested in conveying a content of that order. But that's what they're involved with words for: to get those things said. There are other writers who want to live in their words, like Olson says, "we who live our lives quite properly in print," who want, literally, the experience of realizing themselves in writing, not only to realize themselves but to realize the potentiality and extension of words as a physical event in the world. One of the incredibly nostalgic and poignant situations of Roethke's writing, for example, is that I don't ever feel he came to a person. He looked with deep insistence and longing to find that person, himself, but that person never emerged. I mean it's as if you need to say, will the real Theodore Roethke please stand up? It's intriguing, he's not realized.

André: What about Thomas?

Creeley: Thomas, frankly, to me has always been an extraordinarily muzzy writer. Some years ago Graves offered a reward to anyone who could explicate a poem of Dylan Thomas. I think that was a specious request, but I can well understand his impatience with a kind of smarmy longing that just wanted to hear sweet sounds. Unhappily Dylan Thomas' work contributed to a sense that poetry really doesn't do much of anything except sound rather melodiously in the background; he unwittingly was used as an axe to cut off people who were, you know, I thought far more valuable to writing.

André: Talking about magazines, it often struck me as curious that since there are masses, literally masses of English students and would-be poets that magazines like *Poetry* are never mass-circulation magazines.

Creeley: Well, it may be an awful fact that all of us in various ways have got to realize, that literature is not what it used to be. What I respect increasingly in students is the ability to stop encapsulating an attitude towards writing in the sentimental sense of evaluation: this is a good poem, this is a bad poem. People can speak of writing more ably in terms of linguistics, because the habit of literature has become awfully sentimental. It's like the habit of art history; it tends to get awfully vague. "English Literature" doesn't mean anything frankly. When I taught in Canada, I was teaching a freshman English class in which no Canadian author was required. That's a terrifying estimation of English literature as far as I can judge. I think of people out of Saskatchewan, not sentimentally, but those were real people with a real life event. They'd come from an extraordinarily real place, the Plains, and they'd come in that lovely old-fashioned respect for the educational possibility and they met with the most bleak, scared, spineless subservience on the one hand to the British core of taste and on the other hand to the American economic efficiency, and they fell through the slats.

André: Why did you drop out of Harvard, or do you care to say?

Creeley: I was unable to complete a course in analytic geometry I'd taken as an entering freshman; in the meantime I'd gotten married and gone to India and Burma as an ambulance driver; in other words, so much had changed in my life. It wasn't that I was stupid in terms of mathematical condition or concept. I never had any trigonometry, so I was doing analytic geometry longhand, so to speak; I was doing all that calculation in my head. I could keep up with it in the eagerness of being an entering freshman but not being a jaded and disillusioned last semester senior. Also we'd moved to Provincetown and I was commuting from Provincetown to Boston on one of those lovely old boats like the S.S. *Steel Pier* or the S.S. *Chauncey Depew* and arriving in Boston stoned out of my head because they served liquor on the boat for three hours. I'd lose my books and I was failing, so finally the dean called me in and said, "Look, you have two incompletes and a failure in your three courses and I advise you to withdraw until things are more stable. Then you can come back and finish your last semester." Well, I just never came back, I never really had occasion to. Ten years later I thought of doing it, I had left my first marriage and was thinking of the teaching I had happily found to make a living and I had no degree of any order, and I was being asked to produce one. I eventually went to the University of New Mexico as a graduate student and got an M.A. there. The B.A. from Black Mountain was a euphemism. I told Olson about my dilemma and he said, well, you taught the courses, therefore you should have credit for them—we'll give you a degree. It served. I needed something that would specify I had a particular academic ability.

André: Jack Nicholson's film *Drive, He Said* . . .

Creeley: I could tell you quite a bit about Mr. Nicholson's film.

André: Tell us.

Creeley: Briefly, just after it was shown at Cannes . . .

André: I don't know if everybody knows . . .

Creeley: Jeremy Larner's novel *Drive, He Said* uses as motto, and takes as title a line from my poem called "I Know a Man."

Jeremy is a pleasant man; I was charmed that he liked the poem well enough to use it in that fashion. So three or four weeks ago we were sitting in this room and the phone rang and it was Jeremy calling from Hollywood, saying they'd just completed a film of the novel and the poem was quoted, or more accurately misquoted, and was this all right with me? I was sort of charmed and I said, great, you know; again, obviously, thinking of Tom Clark's sense, why not? Another friend however said, that's ridiculous man; to subsidize Hollywood? So this friend's agent very generously took on the matter for me. The point is, very briefly, the film is a flop. One is not going to get rich on this film or any like it. Finally the whole thing fizzled out; they had no permission to use the title— their previous authorization certainly did not include using the poem in the text of the movie. That's show biz, or rather that's business. To take the thing to court would be both bleak and absurd. I have no final word but I'm sure a small "settlement" will eventually be made plus a free ticket.

André: The film interpreted the important line of the poem as being "the darkness surrounds us." And an academic wrote an essay on the poem as a put-down of those who think the darkness surrounds us. Do you agree with either camp?

Creeley: I don't know. Brautigan told me there was a review in *Time* magazine which quoted the poem, saying the movie was awful but the poem held up pretty well. He also told me, thinking of how quickly things enter public use, there was some report of a swimming competition that began with the headline "Dive, She Said." I can tell you very briefly and quickly "what the poem means to me."

André: Maybe you could read it again.

Creeley: This poem has had a very curious history. Just before I do read it, there was a lovely time once, I think in the early sixties or late fifties, when writing of mine was not usually picked up for critical discussion; in some kind of wild supplement in the London *T.L.S.* there was a weird discussion of this

poem and a poem of Larkin's, "The Whitsun Weddings."
They were talking about the Christian attitude and so on, and
the discussion proposes that the "I" of the poem is probably
Jesus Christ and the John of the poem is probably John the
Baptist. It's the most incredible distortion of any intention I
felt in my . . .

André: Probably got somebody tenure though.

Creeley: Incredible. "John" is almost a hierarchical name for
me, I've had very good friends named John. I was thinking of
one very specific. Instantly two friends occur to me: John
Altoon, a painter who was a very close friend, a very, very
decisive friend for me, and another friend, also a sculptor,
John Chamberlain, who's equally a dear friend. "John" became
a name for an order, of not merely *machismo* or some kind of
campy sense of manhood, but almost a hierarchical name for
some measure of friendship, and a man of that condition.

André: The figure, who I take is largely autobiographical in
The Island . . .

Creeley: Yes, John becomes both myself and the imagination of
a man. It's like John Doe but it isn't, it's like John Bunyan, it's
a hierarchical name.

I Know A Man

As I sd to my
friend, because I am
always talking,—John, I

sd, which was not his
name, the darkness sur-
rounds us, what

can we do against
it, or else, shall we &
why not, buy a goddamn big car,

drive, he sd, for
christ's sake, look
out where yr going.

One thing, the lovely paradox about the movie and everything else is that syntactically the line reads for me

> why not, buy a goddamn big car,
> drive

and *then*

> he sd, for
> christ's sake

André: It is misquoted.

Creeley: Yeah, it's a misquote. The poem protects itself. It didn't even get the syntax straight. Not that I made it simple for them. I like the impulse of "drive," *then* "he said." I could have said, period, you know

> drive. He sd, for
> christ's sake

But "he" doesn't say "drive." I think someone who reads it in the actual impulse will recognize that he isn't saying drive, that's the person who's proposing, "why don't we buy a great big car and drive"; it's the "I" of the poem who is saying "why don't we get out of here," the car being one imagination of how we get from where we're stuck, hopefully to someplace where we won't be. It's the friend who then comes into it, who says, "take it easy, look out where you're going because you can't get out of things by simply driving around." "The darkness surrounds us" was just a kind of confusion and muddiness and opaqueness that people obviously feel in their lives. And this was one sense of "let's get out of this and do something else." The friend just says "look out where you're going" because that impulse is obviously human and to be respected but you don't really do much that way. "I know a man" in the sense, like, I know a man who can fix your roof or like that, a *useful* man to know.

André: You mentioned Richard Brautigan. Are you fond of Brautigan's work?

Creeley: Yes indeed. I think especially fondly of his prose which I didn't take to when I first read it, in Canada actually, when I was in Vancouver, and when I had generously been approached by Don Allen to help with the editing of a selection of prose which was called *New American Story.* Among the materials considered that Don suggested were *A Confederate General from Big Sur* and *Trout Fishing in America.* The latter had been turned down by *x* number of publishers in this country, and Don finally published it. So Don was obviously committed to the writing. I was in a very serious mood in Canada, I don't know why or wherefore, I know one reason was, I had been writing *The Island* and I just couldn't read Brautigan's prose in that state of mind. I mean I read it, I read both novels, this was about 1962 or 3 and I thought they read like some wild shaggy dog story, which in a very real sense they do. But I was too uptight in my own sense of what writing "should" do so that I couldn't read them and I vetoed them—to my everlasting shame because I really dig them. They stick in your head.

André: He seems to be influenced by you.

Creeley: No, I don't—you know who's the actual mentor for Richard's writing, the actual close mentor for his writing is Jack Spicer; he's a very particular student of Jack Spicer's. Speaking of influences, Richard and I were talking about possible editions—I was offered the possibility of editing a selection of Walt Whitman. I had a choice of various authors and the one I frankly was first drawn to was Thomas Wyatt, but then when I actually looked at a text of Wyatt's I realized to fill a book would be pretty difficult; there were extraordinary poems but the range was pretty limited. There are at least a dozen friends I would figure more able, like Ginsberg or Duncan or Zukofsky to do an edition of Whitman, but since I've got the chance, boy that's what I want to do. We were talking about this circumstance, and Richard said he would like to do an active selection of Stephen Crane's poetry, or of poets from the thirties who are largely ignored in this country, like Kenneth Fearing.

André: Yes, I like Fearing.

Creeley: I don't think Richard is interested in so-called melopoeia, he said he wants to say things using the simplest possible unit of statement as the module. The last novel he's published, *The Abortion,* I think is an extraordinary book. I think he's a very particular American writer, he has all the eccentricity of an American of a real order. He's not topical. I was at a friend's house who was reading Tom Wolfe and we were talking about Ken Kesey, and about the time Ken Kesey was at Millbrook at Leary's place and Tom Wolfe's report of the whole impact of that visit; it's a very jazzy and interesting way of saying it, but it's a beautiful journalism. Whereas Richard's writing is initiatory; it's the *primary* statement in his writing that I deeply respect. And his poems again stick in my head; I don't think there's any sense in saying, are they as good as Ezra Pound's? There's no point to that.

André: About predecessors, *The Island* seemed to me to be more like D. H. Lawrence and your short stories seemed to me to be more like James Joyce, which is another of those . . .

Creeley: Lawrence was a really deep influence on me as a younger man. I really thought he was an extraordinary prose writer, *and* poet—the modality in poetry was less of interest to me—especially the short stories, things like "The Fox" and "The Captain's Doll." I really loved his stories. Then Williams had a deep impact on me as a younger writer. Apropos your mention of Joyce, I can literally remember reading *Dubliners* as a junior in high school and the impact that made on me as a *feeling:* incredibly sad. And Stendhal had a like impact—it's hard to say, it's such a meld—Dostoevsky was like God Himself when I was younger. Those were all writers of prose.

Pound is literally instruction. His *ABC of Reading* and a book I used practically as a bible when I was younger, *Make It New,* published by Yale, those books were extraordinarily interesting to me. All of Williams' writing is interesting to me.

Among the so-called Elizabethans, I remember Andrew Crozier asked me what edition of Campion I used and if I was using manuscripts or some edition, and I thought, all I'm using is an anthology that includes some Campion. I remember Campion had a deep impact, I don't know why, just one or two lines that really hit and stuck.

André: How has success hit Richard Brautigan?

Creeley: He's a loner. He grew up in difficult circumstances as a kid; the family had no money and I think his father worked as a fry cook; they moved all around that part of the country, the Northwest, looking for work, two or three months in one place, living in furnished rooms or hotels or motels. Richard came to the city deciding to be a writer, rented a room, watched his money dribble away, he rarely left the room somewhere in North Beach he told me, and then there was a day he decided he had to leave. He hawked everything, got what few possessions he wanted to start hitchhiking, and had a lovely epiphanal moment when he was going through some mountain pass almost at midnight with snowy fields and moonlight and realized only eight hours before he had been in a situation where he thought his life would be more fitly ended. He has had extraordinary response in the last few years which he obviously enjoys. But, for example, when a group in New York approached him with the possibility of making a musical out of one of his novels, guaranteeing him something like $5,000 a month for starters and giving him complete disposition as to what the production should be, Richard really came on the dilemma that that would mean New York productions, Chicago productions, San Francisco productions; it would mean that the actual audience he has in mind for what he writes would basically be excluded; they don't live in New York; they certainly can't pay prices of that order. He realizes that very possibly in ten years he will be a has-been in this vast topical meat-market, so he simply stakes himself as long as possible on present income. He does live in this $75 a month apartment; he told me he had some trouble with a window and his landlord told him that all subsequent repairs on the building will have to be undertaken by the tenants since the building is basically derelict and he doesn't want to put any more money into it. Richard has been married and he has a pleasantly amicable relation with his ex-wife, and with a lovely daughter that he's obviously concerned with. But he's basically a loner. He thinks of coming out here, looking around for a house, but I sense it's going to be rather hard for him to leave San Francisco where he lives across from the big Sears Roebuck on Geary. He's an old friend of Ron Loewinsohn's, and again to my mind, his basic teaching comes from Jack Spicer. He's a westerner. The first time he'd ever been east I think was when he was 35; he'd never been *east* of the Mississippi. Richard told me one last lovely story:—when he got to the Metropolitan Museum, he was charmed by the fact that when he looked at all the lovely Rembrandts his shadow was on the paint. Which ain't ego, it just means wanting to be counted too.

André: Another friend of yours who has sort of entered the "pantheon" is Gary Snyder. Is he around here?

Creeley: He lives up near Nevada City. Richard, now, had been active in the Diggers Community, the Free City and very much in the whole Haight-Ashbury activity before the whole ugliness invaded it. Gary, because of his formal background in Zen, in Tibetan Buddhism particularly, feels a more extensive responsibility to an educational process. He's not particularly interested in teaching in formal institutions, he's very involved in ecological—I suppose we could call them spiritual—states of being. He's just completed building in the last year a lovely house of Japanese design up in the woods above Nevada City. Richard actually will walk around the city and people recognize him or dig him. People want something else from Gary: they want to be instructed, they want to be shown particular disciplines. I don't think they ask that of Richard. Gary's more in the situation of Allen Ginsberg. A different use of it. I mean Allen still stays, I think, like a lovely . . . rabbinical . . . Buddhist.

With Bill Spanos

In all of this, it seemed the most real need underlying was to find some way whereby to have a life with others, find the world we all lived in. One would think it obvious, i.e., just turn left and there you are, but perhaps best put as Allen Ginsberg wrote: "They broke their backs lifting the city to heaven, heaven which is everywhere about them . . . ." Because of the Second World War, because that was what followed the Great Depression, it was hard to believe in the world's general good faith or that the good guys would finally win. So my generation clustered in pockets of dissent, isolated and resistant, until we paradoxically became a curious majority and made the sixties our own.

What were teachers in such a time, or later? Who were they? Much that gets said in all this talking has to do with a sense that the "academic" was perforce the enemy, that, as Williams said in his raging against Eliot, the disaster was he had given poetry "back to the academy . . . ." But Graves was certainly right, that ours is that art for which no academy exists—and possibly that is why poets find such awkward accommodation in the one that seemingly does.

I like the echo Pound takes from Agricola, that poetry's possibilities are to teach, to move and to delight. They go together as Bill Spanos well knows. He has been a teacher who brings his own profound interest to whatever he does, reading or writing or talking. I met him first in Knox College, Galesberg, Illinois, friend of another great teacher, Sam Moon. I guess the question is forever, who was it made it vivid for you, gave you the way in? Here Bill teaches me a lot, quite obviously. Our occasion, a word that gets much use, was his wish to have an interview for the issue of boundary 2 *(Spring/Fall 1978) he'd committed to my work. His editing of that remarkable journal defines whatever one tried here to get said.*

Creeley: I was struck by, you know, coming by that Henry's Frankfurter place where it has the sign out announcing the best Texas hots "in the world or any other place," which is a lovely metaphysical statement.

Spanos: Okay, well, the word "metaphysical," of course, immediately generates all kinds of reverberations these days in talk about poetry . . .

Creeley: It would seem to, yes . . .

Spanos: . . . not only because the New Critics and the early Modernists were tremendously interested in "Metaphysical" poetry but also because Heidegger destroys, that is, deconstructs the metaphysical tradition which is the tradition of Western philosophy. And the key to what's now interesting in the term is etymological . . .

Creeley: Right . . .

Spanos: . . . perceiving *meta ta physika*, that is to say, from after or beyond things as they are . . .

Creeley: Right . . .

Spanos: . . . so that you can see existence all at once inclusively, get the whole picture within the frame of the eye, so to speak . . .

Creeley: Right, some ultimate view of the earth, e.g., from outer space, from some other place that gives the whole pattern.

Spanos: Exactly.

Creeley: Well, I was struck, apropos, it's possibly a digression, but Ihab Hassan a critic, I think works at the University of Wisconsin in Milwaukee, was present at a discussion of science and literature, the *arts*, more accurately, a few years ago at

Temple University. And he was, for example, interested in a persistent sense that he found in a wide spectrum of record from, say, popular literature and/or such activity as pop songs or art songs to people like Chardin, the whole sense of leaving the body as some insistent proposal which in one sense, to my mind, reads as another term of this position of metaphysics, that "place" where all can be seen and/or resolved. And also in reading him later in a discussion in *TriQuarterly*— I was given the magazine by him generously and read it and came upon his discussion of James Joyce and Beckett and the terms "Modern" and "Postmodern" and his point of thinking, from closure of the will to *closure*, the whole pattern of intention in the Moderns, their ability to *see* beyond the world as given to some, not idealization hopefully but a sense of resolution, which would, you know, bring it to a coherence. Therefore Pound's great cry, "I cannot make it cohere" . . .

Spanos: Yes . . .

Creeley: . . . or Yeats' keeps coming back: "Things fall apart; the centre cannot hold . . . ." The sense of failure insofar as the world cannot be made to cohere. Hart Crane is for me an extraordinary Modern artist insofar as he proposes and deliberately attempts a metaphysical resolution of the given world. And by the time we get to Beckett, what Hassan speaks of as the high seriousness of the Moderns has dissipated not literally into cynicism or not even into laughter despite, say, Ionesco or aspects of Beckett, nor has their world view shrunk. It's that the world has become immensely larger or immensely more diverse and immensely more present. And the ability to think it or to bring it into some rational condition has been all but yielded.

In conversations with people at SUNY-Cortland in the late sixties—these were young writers come together for a conference—Olson made a distinction between what he called a poetry of art and a poetry of what he called affect—a f f e c t— and he spoke of himself as being an instance of the poetry of art and, in ways, myself too. But he spoke of such poets as Wieners, John Wieners, as being poets of affect. In so far as the life is the daily life daily lived and its imagination, it wasn't as if it was simply stuck with that but it did not metaphysically propose a conclusion. It wasn't working towards an end in mind. The mind was used to make, the mind was used to not merely to record but to work on what is. "The mind, that daily worker on what is . . . ."

Spanos: Olson— Can I interrupt for a second? Olson in *The Special View of History* has two really great quotations as epigraphs one from Heraclitus and one from Keats. The one from Heraclitus reads "Man is estranged from that with which . . . ."

Creeley: ". . . he is most familiar."

Spanos: Very Heideggerian, by the way . . .

Creeley: Right, right . . .

Spanos: . . . and the second is Keats's great definition of Negative Capability:

> several things dovetailed in my mind, & at once it struck me, what quality went to form a Man of Achievement especially in Literature & which Shakespeare possessed, so enormously—I mean Negative Capability, that is when man is capable of being in uncertainties, Mysteries, doubts without any irritable reaching after fact and reason . . .

Creeley: Right . . .

Spanos: . . . the implication being that we are estranged from that with which we are most familiar because we attempt to name it to coerce it into a metaphysical framework. What I want to say is that what you are suggesting is that there's a kind of sadness about the early Moderns who are developing a recognition, are beginning to recognize that they can't make it cohere, as Pound says in Canto CXVI, and that may be true about the early Moderns whereas the New Critics seem to assume that this is this is the way of encountering existence by way of art. This is what art is and always has been. It's a willful coercion, it's a will to power over existence. Olson obviously is reacting against this impulse to enclose existence. He wants to let it be . . .

Creeley: Well, I was reading this morning, for example, a lovely translation of Basil Bunting's of the opening of Lucretius' *Concerning the Nature of Things* and it has this lovely phrase—Oh wait a minute now—This is actually the fourth section of *Briggflatts* I'm thinking of—Where he says that the sun, that the elements of the earth—And then he gets to the sun, that "the sun rises on an acknowledged land." That to me is the place so to speak in working that I would both recognize and revere. It's an *acknowledged* land. And I love that way of putting it, simply that it's not a land thus coerced, it's not an earth or a world, let's say, that's thus brought to some demanding sense of order. It's an earth found in recognizing its existence. It may seem a more passive attention and it may even seem more uselessly patient. But it's as if the great imaginations of the world that were the gift particularly of the early Moderns, the great Imago Mundi makers—those extraordinary images that Pound and Joyce and Mann or Proust all thus give or equally as Freud— all insist on the sense of a world that would posit it as a case such as this. What's fascinating to me is to see that world so yield so that, say, the persons who would be in effect my elder brothers and sisters or possibly younger uncles and aunts, that is, people as Delmore Schwartz or Randall Jarrell or John Berryman or Roethke or that whole cluster of writers—I was reading them apropos this teaching I'm doing this summer and I see them really *broken* on that painful wheel of trying to sustain a continuing cohering imagination of the world. And not only won't it cohere but it literally breaks in the process. I was reading through some of Jarrell's poetry this morning in the class I'm teaching. It shifts from a wry proposal to the dilemma, the understanding, that the world cannot be thus perceived in its totality. And then it begins to invite, not only to invite but to enforce a disposition towards the very body of persons that becomes terrifying and hostile as, say, with Roethke.

Or the whole insistent theme of existentialism in the forties. I think one aspect of the great modern proposal of resolution of Western thinking came a cropper when abstractions really got "too far out."

Spanos: What you seem to be implying, and I think this is a very interesting point, is that the early Modern poets and even their more recent heirs were sort of tragic in their recognition that the center will not hold, that things do not cohere . . .

Creeley: Right . . .

Spanos: . . . whereas the New Critics begin with the assumption that the task of the poet is positively to impose an order on experience from an "end" (metaphysically). I think, for example, of their commitment to the imperatives of the "fallacy of imitative form." And in this sense of course the New Critics have drastically misread the great early Moderns and lost or concealed their tragic recognition of the terrible and disruptive dynamics of process over against a kind of teleological or metaphysical order.

Creeley: Well, for instance, I keep hearing in the back of my head a phrase Yeats uses in that discussion on Modern poetry where he's talking of his then contemporary sense of writing. He's using as his instances Pound and Eliot, and also Auden, MacNeice and Spender. And his point is, simply, that the hierarchy and order that the past had seemingly given as a mythos and almost as an accumulating sense of factually tribal glory, the great heroes of the continuum of the people and so on, to see these not only yielded but rejected by the young was staggering. He says, now the love of Tristan and Iseult is no more, and hopefully no less, than the fact of the Paddington Railroad Station. And his phrase is "Let us accept the worthless present . . . ." Which is, to me, "Let us accept the actual" as opposed to the, I want to say, the *real,* the real being for me always the imagination. I was talking one time with Jasper Johns about Williams. It was a casual conversation in a car going somewhere. I was talking about Williams' "Only the imagination is real," etc., etc., and was much excited by that, was thinking of it as an attribute in working. And Jasper Johns said, "Oh, I didn't really find the imagination useful. It's a great distraction." You could never imagine a Modernist, a person of the Modern temper saying that whereas the Postmoderns you can absolutely understand why that's said, that imagination constantly posits not possibilities but distracting images as against the initial apprehension.

Spanos: Right. Which gets us, of course, to the *positive* to the *valorizing* of the immediacy of experience. This again connects with what I would call the postmodern impulse. Not only American poetry in Williams' "no ideas but in things" but you know Husserl too, and William James, for that matter, says against the Western metaphysical tradition, "We must return to the things themselves" (*zu den Sachen selbst*). And of course this becomes the fundamental point of departure for Heidegger's phenomenological ontology: the return to the things *themselves*. Which opens up also into what strikes me as being your most pervasive and, in fact, beautiful and potentially significant word in the rhetoric of your poetics: "occasion."

Creeley: Occasion. I keep thinking that as the Latin *occasus* which I always would mistranslate or very often. I couldn't remember whether it was "sun rise" or "sun set." But it's that *occasus* I can't to this day remember whether it's the "rising of the sun" or "the setting." I think it's—anyhow, it's one of them . . .

Spanos: O.K. Let me . . .

Creeley: I was wondering which it is. We should look it up?

Spanos: Let me suggest *this*: that etymologically "Occasion" derives ultimately from the Latin word *cadere* which means "to fall" . . .

Creeley: So it's the "setting of the sun." O.K. I always thought it was . . .

Spanos: Do you know the medieval version of tragic drama called *De Casibus Virorum Illustrium*, "Of the Fall of Great Men"? The way I see it and what strikes me as being so *rich* in this term which you've been using for fifteen years now is that a poetry which derives out of its *occasion*— Olson refers to it as "the act of the instant"—is a poetry which involves the fall into time, into temporality . . .

Creeley: I hear . . .

Spanos: . . . into finiteness. It is a poetry which is oriented, I put this word under erasure, not eastward but westward, not upward not upward but *downward* . . .

Creeley: Right . . .

Spanos: . . . in *beingintheworld*. Like the course of the sun, it's an *occidenting*, so to speak, a westering . . .

Creeley: I hear. I hear. Again, for example, it brings into focus that sense I'd have with Duncan or other poets of my dear company, that sense of being given to write poems as opposed to casting about for various possible themes or subjects, the sense of Olson's, of life as being unrelieved. Or, suddenly, I was thinking of Mallarmé's "A Throw of the Dice," of the word "case," for example: "This is the *case*" and that whole sense that there can be no appeal from anything other than that which is. There can be possible transformations within its terms, or within terms thus reorganized, but there can be no alternatives to that which is. I remember reading P. W. Bridgman years ago—a kind of lovely, dry, clear physicist a long time ago at Harvard. And I loved his sense of time. He was discussing various conceptual senses of time, either with relation to the sciences as in physics but also to various cultural conceptual patterns, and he said, "Of course, the present is that which resolves all other possibilities." That is, the present is that which resolves the past and/or the future. The present is where it comes to be. And that for me, of course, would be the crucial moment. I'd have at times senses like Samuel Beckett's: that instant is so fragily apparent and so often diffuse in its manifestations consciously, let's say, that one very often has the feeling such as "if I had only known" or, you know, things of that order . . .

Spanos: Yes, all right. Listen, again back to the notion of occasion as "grounded" in the fall: the fall is the fall from the One into the . . .

Creeley: into the many . . .

Spanos: It's a dispersal, a dispersal of the logos. Here again the principle of dispersion in Williams' *Paterson*, in Olson's *Maximus*, and in your own poetry—that sense of the disintegration of the One, of the metaphysical One into the many, eternity into time, stasis into process, Being into being, identity into difference. Or, to appropriate from Jacques Derrida, *différance*, where the logos is infinitely deferred, and so where things make a difference and thus the importance of the fragile delicate and disturbing but also tremendously potential, i.e., projective, present.

Creeley: For instance, I was talking the other day in this class I'm teaching. I think that the focus I've been most insistent to have used by various people in the quick summer pattern is to take as two terms, not simple ones at all actually, but simply proposed, the *inside* condition in being in the world, what seems interior, personal to one's life, and the *outside* which could be put loosely as all else or all others and/or all else. And to me, as Olson would say, the cutting edge is always at that place where the inside moves to the outside or confronts the outside or vice versa, that edge where the message of that outside is experienced, is transmitted. In any case, I was suddenly thinking, O.K., you could propose, say, Plato and what derives from his modes of thinking as the process of abstraction and the unity of possible states, the possibility of forms as being unifying and bringing together into a singular condition of experience, the efficacy of forms so proposed and so conceived. And then I said, well, he's a poet, not a poet—He's a thinker therefore primarily of this *inside* state of existence. To me it's instantly interesting that, of course, he does use a cave, though he speaks magnificently of the possibility of getting out of it. It's very interesting to me that he begins with a cave as the imagination of the human place and experience thereof.

Spanos: Yes, that's really significant. It's the fallen world where Idea, eidos, image breaks up into words.

Creeley: So then, on the other hand, one might say there's Aristotle not too long after who's proposing: "What is the nature of the *outside*?" So that his process then becomes an insistent categorizing and naming presumably much involved with the "*It*." You know, consistently a large amount of experience: what is it? But nonetheless we're now thinking—it's as though Aristotle is only maintaining the process that Plato initiates in continuing the authority of forms apart from what else might be even weakly felt to be the case, that is, whether you know it was a bear who bit you or a hyena, nonetheless you've been bitten and *something* did it. And you didn't know it, did you? Like Olson's sense again, that we do what we know before we know what we do. And also that lovely Dylan song, "But you don't know what it is / Do you, Mr. Jones?" You didn't know what "it" was.

Spanos: Kierkegaard, by the way, who is Heidegger's source here, puts it like this: "We live forward and understand backwards." It's the groundless ground of his whole critique of Hegel's Platonic epistemology of Re Collection (of the dispersed One) and, I think, of Heidegger's hermeneutics, i.e., his distinction between a "forwarding" Repetition and backward oriented vicious circularity. It also looks forward, I think, to the postmodern calling into question of a poetry as recollecting in tranquillity (Wordsworth's summary definition) in favor of a projective poetry. In fact, doesn't what you're saying relate to, again, one of those ideas that recurs over and over in Olson—it has for his readers become sort of standard ever since it appeared in Olson's "Projective Verse" but I'm uncertain whether or not most people who read yours or Olson's poetry really understand it: "Form is never more than an extension of content." . . .

Creeley: Yeah . . .

Spanos: Here too it's the . . .

Creeley: See, the dilemma there, as I gather over the years, is pretty precisely in the word "content."

Spanos: Yes.

Creeley: Because for many people the word "content" implies and/or states a sort of mental furniture.

Spanos: Beautiful. That's precisely the hangup that I've encountered in my own teaching of that sentence.

Creeley: I really felt, however vaguely at that point, that it wasn't "content," it was what was in the actual system that could manifest "itself" by whatever form was possible. I mean, the thing that I even then most insistently used as example was the circumstance that *happens*—let's say, what happens when you take a glass of water and just dump it on the floor? The fact of water, the content inherently of water, discovers a form, a form specific to its "nature," to put it loosely, on the surface it meets with. No *idea* of water will change that situation, so to speak. And *that* was the sense of "content" I was proposing, like "murder will out," I suppose, is what I was mostly thinking of, the nature of murder as an act will discover itself not because anyone thinks or wants it to be that way but because *per se* it *is* that way.

Spanos: Again Heidegger, it seems to me, is very illuminating here. At least his is a vocabulary that can illuminate or anyway amplify this notion of content. That is, that he talks about the hermeneutic circle. You know, we know from the end what we're looking for in the beginning but only in a vague way. We know it and don't know it . . .

Creeley: I know, I know . . .

Spanos: It requires not keeping one's aesthetic distance from but leaping *into* the hermeneutic circle totally and primordially if we're going to really find out what we know preontologically, so to speak, but don't know. So that, in Heidegger's terms, in the metaphysical tradition, philosophical and literary, Form (Being) is ontologically prior to process (or temporality), your term content, whereas according to Heidegger's phenomenology and the postmodern poetic impulse, process in your term, content is ontologically prior to Form. In the one, Form like Being is transformed into a substantial entity. In the other, it remains a becoming.

Creeley: I would feel so. We were a few summers ago in company with a young topologist who was working in Cambridge Mass. We were all in Gloucester as it happened. I was asking this friend about various situations of thinking with relation to his work. For one thing I asked him a kind of lovely naive question apropos his sense of his colleagues. I said "Do you find the company thus in working is attractive to you?" I was really thinking of it as a situation of, say, teaching, or writing, for that matter. Did he find a pleasant company in his work? Did he like his coworkers? He said, "Bob, there is no one else in those situations." He said, "I'm thinking," and he meant it not in the least pretentiously, "I'm thinking of the possible cases of something for which there have been no prior postulates, you know, no prior speculation. I'm thinking of the possibilities of this situation's being the case." And he said "The only thing I can refer to my colleagues, as you put it would be the math that's giving me the formulation. In other words, there is no *thing* out there that can constitute agreement, that is, I'm the first person to think *that*." It isn't that he's being grandiose in this proposal. He's literally doing what

Olson proposes, "testing and missing some proof." And it's he has this thing in his mind so he's testing it, like a kid who makes something, who has the imagination of how a thing might be contrived to float on the water, makes it and tries it out. Does it work or doesn't it? It isn't even that he gets necessarily any information back, although possibly either a kid or a topologist would. But again I don't think it would be simply sophistically but to me the content is still generating the form, so to speak, because there isn't anything known until it's thus discovered as possible. And to me the impulse to try to think the world at all would be manifest of a seeming union of content that gets out or as they would say in contemporary jargon gets off in this particular manner. There are obvious uses of this. He was saying, for example, that the structure of waves proves to be in some ways a homologue of the situation of the rapid extinction of dinosaurs. These two "events" in time/space can be shown to have a structure significantly akin. What that then gives one as information is only and interestingly to me a graphing of the experience of knowing nothing more nothing less. It doesn't get you anywhere, does it? It isn't as though one is going anywhere in the nature of thought but one's frankly again discovering where one is, what the specific possibilities of the instrument seem to be. It's that inherent content of the art, it seems to me, that's far more significant than what the art gets to.

Spanos: So that the stance given this orientation, if you will . . .

Creeley: Bill, it's almost as if one is trying to propose and, hopefully, understand if it's still possible to be human in your mind.

Spanos: O.K. The way I would put it is like this. The stance given this orientation is *beingintheworld.* That's what being human is: being-in-the-world. You can't stand outside it. You've got to be *interested.* Kierkegaard plays on the etymology of this word "interest" so devalued by the Western metaphysical tradition, *inter esse*, in the middle of, in between. You've got to—I'm going to invoke the central term in Heidegger's *Being and Time*—you've got to be *careful* . . .

Creeley: Yeah . . .

Spanos: . . . and of course in "Letter 5" of *The Maximus Poems,* the letter addressed to Ferrini, Olson focuses on two radically related words that crop up both in his and your poetry and prose over and over again pervasively, along with words like "occasion." "You see," he tells Ferrini whom he can't "meet" because like his poetry magazine *4 Winds* he's placeless, and thus careless, "You see I can't get away from the old *measure* of care . . . ."

Creeley: Olson says, that men might care about the kind of world they live in, his respect for Winthrop, for example, as against John F. Kennedy, who uses Winthrop's words . . .

Spanos: Yeah.

Creeley: . . . when he addresses the Massachusetts legislature prior to his becoming president and invokes Governor Winthrop's previous address to that body when he says, at one point, he wants "that city to shine upon its hills." And Olson's point is that men as Winthrop did then *care* about the kind of world they lived in. And the dilemma at present is that as the human collective we no longer care about the collective fact of the world in which we live. So that for Olson, I think very distinctly in his case and in mine, our anger, though I speak for myself, our anger against a poet such as Robert Frost would be that neither one of us believed he *cared*, that he was quite agreeable to the appropriation of the situation of New England as condition of people and circumstance historically, but otherwise he factually didn't give a damn. As Olson, for example, in like sense does truly attack Pound. He said, "As they also, / with much less reason, from too much economics speak / of the dream / in a peasant's bent shoulders, as though it were true / they cared a damn / for his conversation . . . ."

Which is to say, they don't *care* about this man or this place. They use him or it as a symbol of some cultural fact but the actual instance of the person or place they have no interest in whatsoever.

Spanos: And this is connected too in a fundamental sense with the New Critical commitment to aesthetic distance. You've got to transcend the occasion. You've got to rise above it so you can see the whole picture at once, *meta ta physika*. When you write your poem, it must not emerge from its occasion. It must not in Olson's terms be the "act of an instant." You can't care. You can't *care*. You can't write poetry in *care*, *interestedly*. You've got to stand outside the occasion objectively so that you can form it, so you can *shape* it, which is to say coerce it, from an *end*.

Creeley: Well that to me again would be a hopeful kind of neoplatonic act . . .

Spanos: Precisely.

Creeley: . . . that wants to leave life by thinking about it. For example, visiting in southeast Asia a year ago last spring, in South Korea as it was actually, I found a whole tradition of teaching which has been there a long time in which a teacher stands responsible to his or her students forever after in relation to their information as against, say, our Western tradition where we make continuing friendships with students possibly but we certainly don't feel necessarily responsible for the information they were or were not given. Whereas in the Korean pattern the teacher stands forever after as pledge for that information he is responsible for in his student's training. And that student is absolutely free to recall him to it and/or to demand that he continue the instruction if something seems missing in the situation. There's no sense of "Look kid, you graduated. I'm busy now with these other guys." I suppose there are still aspects of this in the European tradition, of handing on the information to a particularly gifted student rather than just broadcasting it and hoping someone will pick it up. But again it's the nature of care, that one finds in the Korean sense of responsibility such as I think Duncan defines when he says that for him responsibility is the ability to respond. He doesn't mean that cynically or glibly. He means literally that that's what to him responsibility constitutes, a factual response whether to something read, seen, felt or heard, but, very primarily, to other persons. Again in that long and extraordinary friendship with Olson I was very, very aware in his writing but equally in his conversations or all else, that he really disliked an abstraction that wanted to be apart from that which it observed. I think that's why those persons in my generation, friends as Allen Ginsberg, were delighted by Heisenberg. We would chant almost as a mantra, "Observation impedes function!" I was told many times by friends who were physicists that that wasn't what Heisenberg had in mind. But we didn't care. We loved the sense of "Aha! You see, if you attempt that discrete distance from the thing happening, you will literally not only not get such an actual view of it or actualizing view of it—you very possibly won't get into it at all!" Then too in college I recall taking very briefly courses in cultural anthropology and coming upon such delicious terms as "participant observation" and then being told by Clyde Kluckhohn, who was teaching such a class, that his sister Jane had got into an extraordinary dilemma by "participating" and "observing" in a "cultural rite," I think, of the Navajos in which she discovered she was momently to be married if she didn't take more care, so to speak. She was an extraordinary lady without exception. But I mean, had she been less observant and more participating, she probably wouldn't have been in that fix to begin with. So that, in other words, I question that we can get it so together in our thinking of it that we don't need otherwise to be *there*.

Spanos: Again of course the New Critical stance is the stance of disinterestedness, *dis*interestedness, and it goes by the term "objectivity." The poet, and the reader or critic, according to this aesthetic perspective, should be objective. And, of course, that term is very crucial because it makes the experience being articulated by the poet an *object*. It *object*ifies or, in my terms, it *spatializes* existence, which is processual, which is temporal, and can't finally be taken hold of, manipulated . . .

Creeley: See, Bill, for example, what may be a very specious parallel but if one sits, say, in a usual small city court for so-called petty criminals and sees the disposition of the "objective" judge vis à vis these persons and sees otherwise the conduct of a judge who is less abstract, one *knows* who is really being useful. But that kind of "objective" use of intelligence or perspective would be very useless I think. In other words, a doctor considering some patient who has a particular disease understandably doesn't *necessarily* want to be involved with the person as person. He wants to say if you do this or that you'll find yourself recovering from this particular illness. But then I've been told by doctors also that one of the hardest things professionally to remember is that at a time when humanly the doctor's resources are possibly *most* useful is when he feels he has none, e.g., when the patient is going to die. This doesn't at all mean that he or she should take over the role of the possible priest or the person thus able to ritualize that information. But it does mean that no information is abstract, that you *don't* say, "Well, Bill, you've got terminal cancer and now it's time for me to go home. I can't do anything for you." A criticism that proposes to be apart from that which it actually is involved with is to me totally absurd. I cannot believe . . .

Spanos: . . . or the writing of poetry . . .

Creeley: I want to say almost didactically that there is no information that does not have an affective content, even if it's blinking lights or numbers in random series.

Spanos: This, of course, activates at least in my own mind another very central metaphor, which is so basic to Olson, to your poetry, to the poetry that emerges out of Williams and Pound the notion of poetry as discovery the notion of poetry as *periplus* . . .

Creeley: Yes . . .

Spanos: "Not as . . . ." How does Pound put it in Canto LIX?

> periplum, not as land looks on a map
> but as sea bord seen by men sailing.

And you've seen those old maps where the process of discovery is immediate, is *local*, and its affective impact is *there* in the goddamned exaggerations, the "distortions," of the line, which are more real, so much more real, than the map, that homogenized and domesticated space seen from that disinterested, technological distance of the map maker, who draws it from his desk, his metaphysical desk, so to speak. This is why again Olson's metaphor of Juan de la Cosa in *Maximus* is so crucial to the postmodern context. He celebrates Columbus' cartographer and his mappemunde because, unlike Martin Behaim, *he was there.* The title says it all: "On first Looking out through Juan de la Cosa's Eyes." You pick this up not in terms of the metaphor of Juan de la Cosa but of seeing things freshly. You make a lot of it in a number of your essays on Olson and all over the place in *A Quick Graph* . . .

Creeley: Yeah, I love that: "He left him naked / the man said . . . ."

Spanos: Right. It's what Husserl calls the "phenomenological reduction."

Creeley: Yeah—

> He left him naked,
> the man said, and
> nakedness
> is what one means
>
> that all start up
> to the eye and soul
> as though it had never
> happened before

Spanos: Exactly: "as though it had never / happened before . . . ." And of course this generates an attitude towards the antitheses, which everyone is kicking around these days ever since Derrida. In deconstructing Heidegger himself started to devalorize speech in favor of writing, *parole* in favor of *écriture* . . .

Creeley: The thing . . .

Spanos: That is to say, goddamnit, what the epistemological stance of Williams and Pound and Olson and you and so many other younger contemporary poets generates is a poetry that is fundamentally "the cry of its occasion / Part of the res itself and not about it." That's Wallace Stevens' phrase from "An Ordinary Evening in New Haven" but it applies so much more it seems to me to the kind of poetry that you're "writing," a poetry, that is to say, which has its "source" in the speech act as opposed to writing, as opposed to the poem as something you compose for the printed page . . .

Creeley: I was thinking this morning in talking to my people— I'd asked them to bring to class any particular poem that seemed to them an instance, hopefully an extraordinary instance, of the possibilities of poetry as an art, something that was dear to them, something provocative to their own senses of the possibility of writing, something that constituted for them a measure of its resources and possible glory. And I was struck that only about five or six thus brought in texts. Three of those five or six were translations and rather indifferent translations. So that the initial, say, active composition of the poem had already been diluted once and they didn't seem to be dismayed that this was the case. This was the process of objectifying. Here was the poem initially. It had been objectified by the translation, that is, abstracted. They were reading it in that situation and I remember I kept saying: "Well, what about some situation of first consciousness as a possibility?"— admitting that you could have an instance of translation which actually was far more interesting than the poem initially, possibly Mallarmé's translation of the "The Raven" by Edgar Allan Poe, which might be thought *more* interesting as a poem than Poe's. And Pound's translations seem to me very possibly so. But in any case, what I'm trying to say is, I read to them not aggressively but from my own interests. I read them Bunting and I read them Patrick Kavanagh. And I love Patrick Kavanagh's poems although I know them, frankly, very poorly. I mean, I haven't literally got a book of his in the house, which it seems to me is not happy. Because I'm *really* attracted to him. And I recall when Olson got back from an International Festival of Poetry in London. I think it must have been around 1968 or '69, it was around that time, possibly a little later. I asked him what poets in that situation had interested him and he said the two most deliciously extraordinary poets, in fact, in some ways the *absolute* poets of the occasion were Ungaretti and Patrick Kavanagh. He said what was so extraordinary about both men was that they read in no literary disposition. Their writing was in no way attached to a literary politics as was the writing of Auden, for example, or rather more sweetly the writing of Spender or frankly the writing of others who were therefore involved. He said neither person read or thought of poetry as anything more than *this act*. And the honor they felt *in* the art was extraordinary. He said Ungaretti read an *extraordinarily* simple poem of the seasons. It was sort of an incredibly sweet breeze blowing through this rather tepid and constricted group. A *very* simple human act of recognition so calmly and commonly put that your mind is literally blown away by its beauty.

Spanos: I get the sense, by the way, of something like this in a number of the poems that you sent me from Spain which hopefully will get included in this special issue of *boundary 2*. There are several of those which are so fundamental, so basic, so naked as perceptions:

> Across bay's loop
> of white caps,
> small seeming black
> figures at edge—

one, the smallest,
to the water goes.
Others, behind,
sit down.

And the whole notion of the literary context simply doesn't apply, is not applicable except in the sense that someone who knows poetry brings to bear upon his reading those habitual formal expectations of the tradition which are being undercut, called into question by the freshness, the nakedness, of the perceptions and the language that expresses them . . .

Creeley: I was at the Cambridge Festival in April, '77 and the people who really moved and delighted me there were of two basic kinds. They were either those like Tadeusz Rozewicz, the Polish poet, who were absolutely facts of human experience, of having lived a life in a particular event, e.g., the Second World War and the subsequent political/social reality. They were not proseletizing in any usual or glib way. They were saying "I bear witness." There were extraordinary poems of that order, constantly preoccupied with being, staying, knowing the condition of being in a world that was so often hostile and bleak. They were very moving as such. That nature of poetry such as was there was to my mind very dear. And the other was where there was some absolutely extraordinary preoccupation with, I'm going to say, the material conditions of the language itself as in the work of the Frenchman Jean Daive, then a beautiful younger Scots poet Thomas H. Clark, who writes with such a modesty and clarity that it's really lovely, it's sweet and again it has this lovely fresh appetite as opposed, sadly, to writers who are much of my generation like Geoffrey Hill, the *Mercian Hymns*, for example, which are so heavy. I would not denigrate his own abilities as a poet at all but I would wonder if in that world, let's say, their particular valuing is not as much a situation of literary politics as it is an actual event.

Spanos: I've been reading his poems recently because someone, Merle Brown from the University of Iowa, in fact, came to Binghamton this spring and read an interesting paper on his poetry. I must say though that I find Hill's poetry very "literary" with little real awareness of what I would call the crisis of poetry or at any rate with little inclination to interrogate, to radically interrogate the forms and the rhetoric he's received from his immediate forebears. And in this sense though it's powerful in many ways, his poetry is a throwback to another time, really to Modernism.

Creeley: I could much respect, say, a possibly purely literary poetry, that is, a poetry that uses as its material all the accumulations of reading and writing that had been witnessed or got to, that was deliberately, not deliberately but was possibly unintentionally cranky in that way. Some quick parallel might be a kind of hermetic artist like Joseph Cornell using incredible allusions and echoes of previous events and patterning in making thus his own work. But I found the disposition in too many of the writers there, I mean it was like people hustling for authority in a rather meager spectrum of event. Another poet I found extraordinarily otherwise was actually the one poet I think that Basil Bunting ever specifically both husbanded and took on as an active protégé, Tom Pickard. And it's just as Robert Duncan was saying—we were both there— the actual delight in the power of this art without the least sentimentality is so distinct when you meet with it. And Tom Pickard has that power. And he takes care of it. Again he has as Olson would say, "both the attention and the care." But he of all people would know that you don't learn it in the usual manner. You practice it and you take care in the practice and learn through the practice but you don't acquire it. It's not a quantitative information. And again it comes from living a life unrelieved. I mean, going for broke, I'd like to say, in all possible situations in one's experience and not always thinking, "Will this be the poem appropriate to the literary political climate of the moment?" etc. Bunting I find an extraordinary poet in that way. He's now 77. And of all the poets I've ever known I don't think one's lived a life more precisely and humanly committed in all respects. I mean he's a poet with absolute distinction. At the same time his life has not been caught in that singular attention. By which I mean all his life feeds that process and all that process feeds his life. And he won't go to Cambridge or Oxford any longer. He finds them really distasteful. He one time said there was a time when Oxford would hire a person because of his or her information about a particular area of human activity or whatever increment. That is, you would be given a situation or a professorship at Oxford in the late 1800s because you knew something. Now it's only because you "studied" it in a particular school.

Spanos: Basil Bunting was at SUNY-Binghamton in the spring of . . .

Creeley: I know. He was . . .

Spanos: And a very unhappy experience he had there. No one, neither faculty nor students with the exception of Milt Kessler, was responding to his presence. He was, I think, outside their frame of reference, their received understanding of Modern poetry.

Creeley: It's sad . . .

Spanos: It's very sad, though, I must say, near the end of his visit he read *Briggflatts* with the Scarlatti background which was one of the most stunning readings I have ever encountered in my life. It was absolutely magnificent.

Creeley: Apropos of the failure to respond to his presence he presents his information at times so casually that if you're not particularly aware of either the persons or the situation he's recalling, you think he's just another older man wandering on about what happened to him some years ago when you weren't born. But if you start listening to what he's actually talking of and about and to what purpose, he's an absolutely extraordinary man. I think he's lived the human life as successfully as any man I've met.

Spanos: What you're talking about in fact brings up another term that is pervasive in your vocabulary, critical and poetic, and that is the word "measure." Now the word "measure" applied to the poetic tradition recalls at least in my mind the Platonic or, more broadly, the logocentric notion of music held dear by the Elizabethans and insistently invoked by the Metaphysical poets as it began to disintegrate the notion of music in which measure is absolutely determined by perceiving "meta ta physika," from God's eye, so to speak. I'm thinking, for example, of Ulysses' speech about the untuned string in Shakespeare's *Troilus and Cressida* or Sir John Davies' *Orchestra*:

> Dancing, bright Lady, then begins to be,
> When the first seeds, whereof the world did spring,
> The fire, air, earth, and water did agree,
> By Love's persuasion, nature's mighty king,
> To leave their first disordered combating,
>   And in a dance such measure to observe
>   As all the world their motion should preserve.

But obviously what you're doing to that word so conceived is deconstructing it. You're making that word mean something very different from what it has meant in the logocentric tradition.

Creeley: It's—See again one tends to get locked into the circumstance of what does it mean to me. Perfectly relevant and useful question. However, there would seem to me necessary some acknowledgement in Bunting's sense, that is, as sun rising on an acknowledged land, that the *me* is not the only term of that situation's reality, much as being told as a kid, "Don't play with the cat that way, you're going to hurt it." I mean the cat has a life too and you have to humanly recognize that, that you can't live in an egocentric world entirely. So that measure again really comes back to Olson's sense of "testing / And missing / some proof." I've recalled, for example, in a book like *Words* what seemingly, in large part unconsciously, was on my mind, was what is it in the world that permits a measure of the world? What can one use as not objectification but as locus? How do you locate? Location, it seems to me, is a much more useful word than—I mean, where is it? How is it? What is it? When is it? All of those kinds of questions. If I'm in some respects the control term, if I'm that which it acts upon and that which in turn acts upon it, what are the ways in which I know it? And how can I therefore posit it as existing? Insofar as I know it exists, I both intuit and recognize its existing. This was what was fascinating to me in Wittgenstein's contest with Moore over Moore's "empirical epistemology." Moore satisfied himself by saying, "O.K., the tree exists, i.e., I can go up and put my hand on it. Therefore" you know almost like Bishop Berkeley "it exists insofar as I experience its existing." And Wittgenstein instantly said, "Well, this would be all very well if one could posit oneself as such a reliable index. But then maybe you *didn't* see it, or maybe it fooled you. It *wasn't* a tree, it was an elephant's leg or something." So that I didn't want, let's say, to put myself into an increasingly abstract situation of experience, which was frankly my tendency as a young man—to become more and more abstract. Whenever I'm talking with persons who are involved with, say, human behavior psychologists or psychiatrists, the thing they remark instantly apropos of my ways of saying things or of expressing myself is that my habits in that expression are very abstract. I mean I tend to be very abstract. It isn't that I'm avoiding the "subject." But I tend to think around it or to enclose it so as a thing thought that the feelings otherwise the case are curiously muted or diffuse. They, of course, might well say, "But you may be only coloring the poems." And, of course, there they have me because I think I wrote the poems in some experience of feeling. But all I have as evidence is the poem and I can't argue any more than they can whether it's an artifact of feeling or whether it's an artifact of thought. I don't particularly want to make the judgment. It really gets locked in a honeyhead, so to speak. I was reading Coleridge these last few weeks apropos of a friend's thesis. God, the dilemmas of abstract thought are just terrifying. You see where the sad agency of opium addiction plus an extraordinarily articulate mind could land in existence.

Spanos: Keats said, and again I'm sure Olson was very much aware of it, that Coleridge through his obsessive abstractness, his "irritable reaching after fact and reason," his lack of Negative Capability, of being able to remain "in uncertainties, mysteries, doubts," missed Shakespeare, "would let go by" beautifully ironic words, "a fine isolated verisimilitude caught from the Penetralium of mystery . . ."

Creeley: It seems to me he sadly missed the very significance of his own composition, e.g., "The Rime of the Ancient Mariner," in which the accretions are very interesting. What he does is to add to it, in short. And they're interesting. But I wonder if he actually knew not so much what he was doing, but I wonder if he wasn't working on the poem as an artifact as opposed to expanding the poem as an information. I wonder if he thought he was making it better in some diminished sense. When Wordsworth suggested he leave it out in the second edition of the *Lyrical Ballads*, he apparently made no objections. He felt it was quite reasonable.

Spanos: To come back to "measure"— For Plato again music— *Mousike*—and by extension measure is very crucial. Now similarly, or let me put it this way, one of the problems I have with Olson's *Maximus Poems* is the tremendous valorizing of the eyes—

> polis is
> eyes
> . . . .
>
> Eyes,
> & polis,
> fishermen,
> & poets
>> or in every human head I've known is
>> busy
> both:
> the attention, and
> the care
> . . . .
>
> so few
> have the polis
> in their eye . . .

Creeley: And he ends—

> There are no hierarchies, no infinite, no such many as mass,
> there are only
> eyes in all heads,
> to be looked out of

Spanos: Right—and, of course, in the metaphysical tradition since Plato, the eye has been valorized over all the other senses. This is a point, by the way, that Heidegger makes over and over again in his destruction of Western philosophy. Obviously Olson means something very different in his appeal to the eye and you mean something different in valorizing the eye. But how would you rationalize the—or how would you interpret the similar emphasis he gives to vision and hearing, the eye and the voice? Is it the eye in the sense of self, e.g., "I see," which is the . . .

Creeley: No. I think it's the factual, physical, like Zukofsky's physical eye. I think what attracts Olson is that the eye is the primary sense for the function of a primate, that the eye is the crucial input factor. For the poet hearing then comes very, very insistently as another, crucial sense. It's the collector. It's where the phenomenality of the outer world can—where that information can be gathered, the agency of the ear. *Previous* to thought—I think that's the point, that, again, the eye doesn't *know* what it sees. It sees it primarily.

Spanos: I understand. In other words whereas in the tradition in Plato the whole object is to transform the entire body, *all* the senses, into one all-perceiving or re-collecting eye, i.e, so that the world becomes spatialized . . .

Creeley: Yeah, but see that's . . .

Spanos: . . . Olson, in contrast, is really de-constructing, isn't he, that Platonic notion of *encompassing* eye and integrating the eye in a much closer relationship to the other bodily functions?

Creeley: He was fascinated by the scientific proposal that the photocells in the skin were like little eyes . . .

Spanos: Oh yes, beautiful. Merleau-Ponty talks about the incarnate knowledge of the body.

Creeley: . . . that all of them were capable of individual adaptation, that the physical surface of one's body was a dense cluster of minute photocells all having the possibility of that consciousness in the singular . . .

Spanos: Where does he refer to this in his writing? Or is it something he said to you?

Creeley: It seems to me he does somewhere. I can't quickly recall, possibly in *Proprioception*, but more possibly in that "Human Universe" piece, where he's talking about judgment and recognition. He insisted, for example, and I thought, usefully, that judgment is instant upon recognition, that the moment you see something your response to it is judgment. You don't wait to think about it. You may revise that judgment or alter it but your first response to recognizing it is an immediate judgment. But to come back specifically to your question about Olson's sense of eyes . . .

Spanos: I wasn't asking the question about eyes in any gratuitous way because in that crucial phrase from the *Maximus Poems* he uses two terms which are central to Plato and the whole Western, Heidegger calls it the onto-theological, tradition: "Polis / is eyes . . . ."

Creeley: It's almost as though he tacitly wants to correct Plato by saying "Polis *is* eyes." It isn't an abstract situation of eyes, it's an absolute or functional activity of eyes. People are, again, literally physical function. As he says, "There are only eyes in all heads to be looked out of." There isn't any more. "There is no such many as the mass." "There is no hierarchy" etc., etc. There is no system which can supersede or otherwise be the case but the factual existence of these human beings with the factual possibility of their senses, e.g., literally their eyes that can see. He *loved* the idea of "to bear witness." One time years ago when we were first corresponding, he had come upon, I think, a very primary, he proposed it even as the first, instance of recorded speech. I want to say it was previous to Sumerian. In any case, the first record he was thus proposing as being the first to me was simply the statement of, apparently, the foreman of a mine shaft saying, "I, John, foreman of Mine Shaft X do say this." And he loved it, that the first recorded speech, as he was therefore thinking of it, was an instance of such "bearing witness." This was directly an instance of bearing witness. "I have seen this. Mine eyes have seen the glory." So it isn't abstract or symbolic, it's factual, literal. He loved it the same way he loved that sense of Herodotus' going to take a look for himself . . .

Spanos: "I would be an historian as Herodotus was, looking / for oneself for the evidence of / what is said . . . ," he says in "Letter 23" of the *Maximus Poems*. He also makes a great point of that Herodotan impulse in the *Special View of History*.

Creeley: Because to him there was no alternative, as he put it, to the going on that "what happened" would have to be absolutely the the experience of it. There had to be the witness of it. And you got the witness of it through the transfer, then, of that experience. That is, I could tell you what I had seen and you would have it in that way then too. But neither of us could have it unless one of us had actually . . .

Spanos: It's the perspective of Juan de la Cosa again, the Poundian *periplus* again, in phenomenological vocabulary the perspective after the phenomenological reduction . . .

Creeley: Yeah. One time, when we were all living up in Vancouver in the early sixties, just by beautiful chance watching TV one evening, suddenly we were watching and listening to a conversation between Stefansson, the Arctic explorer, and a now also quite old sea captain, a Swede, who had been one of the men that had helped transport Stefansson up to this place in the Bering Straits, in that northern area. And they were recalling the difficulties, physically of transporting men and supplies in that part of the world, the freezes in the winter, and the difficulties of just being there at all. And then, this beautifully, absolutely unanticipated, nostalgic moment, they started recalling the *look* of a particular bay there and it was *delicious*. I mean, you knew that possibly a half dozen persons from our world would ever see that place at all. But suddenly these two had this extraordinarily—Not just nostalgic but this beautifully alert situation: "You *saw* it too!" Just this extraordinary moment of a *communicated* sense of sharing . . .

Spanos: That's polis . . .

Creeley: That's "polis / is eyes . . . ." Right. There is no bond other than that . . .

Spanos: And the poem too is polis isn't it? The poem as analogy of the experience of community as bearing witness . . .

Creeley: Yeah, and lovely in a sense that Ginsberg makes clear. He one time was saying that his poems are a kind of curious time capsule insofar as you can open them later and have the information as, say, someone else, those "recorders ages hence" in Whitman's sense or Stendhal's. I can read *now*, at this "point" in time and space, and share, literally participate in, the emotions that were Ginsberg's being *there and then*. I feel that. Like a friend in England has been sending us potsherds and coins that he discovers very casually in the field adjacent to where he lives outside of Cambridge. And these are coins dating back to about 200 B.C. And the coins are the classic penny kind of coin and you can *feel* them, you know, the Roman soldiers probably just dropping small loose change out of their pockets, like the *substance* of the potsherds you can suddenly feel the human condition, the hand, you can really—It isn't sentimental but you can actually feel it . . .

Spanos: Apropos of this you've got to read if you haven't already "The Origin of the Work of Art" by Heidegger because he talks about Van Gogh's painting of a number of paintings that he did of a peasant's pair of shoes and you know he's saying virtually the same thing about them that you are about the coins and the potsherds . . .

Creeley: It's hard indeed not to almost instantly, for me at least, to sentimentalize those moments. But the very few times when I, again always without plan, suddenly became present to it. It's so extraordinary, e.g., one time in southern Mexico, up in San Cristobal, we were driving through going down to Guatemala where I was to teach, and we stopped to pay respects to an old time kind of adventurer self-styled anthropologist named, oh gosh, he was a Dane—Actually as I recall, *Bloom.* He was called Peter Bloom, anyhow his last name was Bloom. But in any case we were talking. He had this lovely kind of showman's style with his information. His place was now being used as a primary staging situation for expeditions into the peninsula. So the University of Chicago and Harvard's Peabody Museum, its persons, were all there getting his advice and maps and stuff to go in. Pancho Bloom—*Franz Blum* was his name. So, in any case, he said, "How would you like to meet a Mayan?" I said, "Terrific!" He said, "Actually the man is a Lacandon Indian. He's the first person ever to come out of his particular situation, ever. The first human being of that particular cluster ever to go beyond its stated boundaries and to move out of its area of habitation into this world." And I said, "That would be an honor indeed if in my American sense it wouldn't bother him. If it wouldn't be an imposition upon him, I would be honored to meet such a human being." And so he said, "He's in the next room, I'll ask him to come out." So momently here was this man, another human being, standing there and in no sense "primitive" in the sense that his teeth were filed, the sometime imagination of the primitive caveman, just another extraordinary human being. I did again the American thing of putting out my hand. And he looked at it and then, and I was very relieved, he took it. What was extraordinary about this man was that *all* the senses were absolutely alert all over the body in the same way you'd experience the situation of a so-called wild animal as opposed to a domestic animal. I mean the sensory system was absolutely alert, not worried but he was entirely there. I've never met a human being who was so completely *where* he was, not that he knew where he was or was determined to stay there, but he was absolutely alive in the moment of each instant. I mean, there was no abstraction in him. It was fantastic. I thought, "You can do it." I mean you can arrive at a consciousness that's present as opposed to one that's thinking about what happened last week or what is going to happen tomorrow as an imposition on the present instant. Extraordinarily fresh. He was healthy and, as one might expect, his whole sensory nervous system was absolutely incredible.

Spanos: Olson makes this observation about the Mayans in the *Mayan Letters*, doesn't he? . . .

Creeley: In a somewhat like sense, as a younger man during the war and coming into contact with the Ghurkas, their central nervous system was fantastic. They again had not as purely, let's say, as this Lacandon Indian, but they had two aspects of that same centering of physical being without consciousness of being otherwise. So that when they were given things like sodium pentathol as an anaesthetic—the average Caucasian, the average European or American, will tend to go out certainly by ten in the countdown. Most people are anaesthetized by the time they get to eight or nine. These men have been known to count to a hundred. I mean, they have a central nervous system that just won't quit. It's far beyond any of ours. I've seen operations rather horribly performed on these men when in all respects they should have been long gone with shock. I saw a man thus in his sixties walking out of the jungle after having been hit three times by .45 caliber bullets, two of them right through the solar plexus. No European presumably would have survived that. It seems to be not the mental integrity but the *corporeal* integrity of human beings that's extraordinary. I know that Olson, for example, wanted as he said to write a book of the body. And again and again, as I'm reading these various texts of poetry, say from Whitman's time to the—Not to the present actually but to the forties and fifties, the crisis seems to be endlessly the awful success of the process of objectivity and abstraction. So that the mind seems to have almost no consciousness of the body it lives in, even when it's seemingly preoccupied with it, as in, say, Roethke, where the verse is at times almost so wistfully, naively childlike. I think of Roethke's poem about himself and his father dancing, and moving this bearish, this strong, factually quite strong, physical human being that thinks of himself as being so but can't think himself back into the body from which he's separated.

Spanos: I think immediately in contrast of that poem by Williams where he—"Danse Russe," is it? Where he dances naked in front of a mirror and so becomes, as a bodily entity, the divinity of the household . . .

Creeley: Yes. That's a beautiful poem.

Spanos: Oh that's such a marvelous thing. Let me read it:

> If I when my wife is sleeping
> and the baby and Kathleen
> are sleeping
> and the sun is a flame-white disc
> in silken mists
> above shining trees,—
> if I in my north room
> dance naked, grotesquely
> before my mirror
> waving my shirt round my head
> and singing softly to myself:
> "I am lonely, lonely.
> I was born to be lonely,
> I am best so!"
> If I admire my arms, my face,
> my shoulders, flanks, buttocks
> against the yellow drawn shades,—
>
> Who shall say I am not
> the happy genius of my household?

All right. Let me ask you how this suspension of the knowledge of the mind in favor of a knowledge of the body, so to speak, translates into your own poems. I think I can see it operative all over the place, in the form as well as the content of your poetry, but I'd like to hear how you yourself conceive of that translation.

Creeley: Well, there's the world. And living in the world, there are things. Things come to mind or come to be said, or feelings constantly not so much fluctuate although they did immensely when I was younger—But it's my belief if not my understanding that very little I plan to do is as interesting as what I *do* do. In fact, I don't think *anything* I plan to do is as interesting as what I do do or what comes thus to happen. I don't feel that it's therefore stupid to make the obvious plans of usual life, that is, plans to get to bed at a certain time if you're going to get up early in the morning, or plans to have enough money in hand to do whatever. I don't think that kind of provision is stupid at all. But the sense of designing one's life, or of having an overriding intention with respect to one's life, seems to me to be pretty tacitly, if not absolutely overtly, disastrous. I'm struck, for example, with someone as T. S. Eliot. When asked about his intentions with respect to *The Waste Land* he can answer quickly and clearly to the effect that intention is not a word he would use with respect to poetry, certainly not with respect to his own poems nor, frankly, to any poems of his interest . . .

Spanos: I think, in fact, that *The Waste Land* has been entirely misunderstood in that respect. I mean critics, especially the New Critics despite their "intentional fallacy," have read the poem as if its structure was somehow pre-planned. It's worth saying in passing that this is one of the poems in the canon of Modernism that desperately needs deconstructing . . .

Creeley: The critics of that time presumed Eliot had a "plan" but the fact that Pound edits the initial text into the poem they are reading really makes your point very clearly. What happens is so much more engaging and compelling and useful to me in the human condition than what was supposed to happen as an intention. So I would think of my writing as a kind of manifest of not so much again Olson would be dismayed when persons wanted to identify Maximus as being an egocentric projection of his own values of himself. And he'd say, "No! No! No! It's simply a possibility of material. I mean it's 'me' because *I'm* here, this thing is here, so it's my agency for the recognition of what else is here. I'm the *material* of my poem, I'm not the center of it in some egocentric demand." That to me makes absolute sense as did Marisol, the sculptor, saying, "Working alone at night I had no other model so I used myself." I would use myself in a like sense. I wouldn't particularly value myself more or less. I don't know at times if I don't get stuck in some false humility because I do have pride in what I can at times do. And I have as Basil Bunting would emphasize a conscious sense of craft. But I do know also that in writing I have more the *habit* of this activity than I do the conscious decision of it. It would be like asking a tennis player in mid-act why he thought to do that at that moment. I don't know that I could respond. It seems to me that a lot of attention has been given it, but I don't know that I have the conscious decision always of what I thus collect as information. It seems to me to be much more able if it isn't interrupted by some *insistently* conscious decision apropos its use. I know that, say, during the Vietnam war I wanted insistently to write something specifically involved with that political horror. It just didn't work. The moment the will enters, for me it gets really muddy and difficult . . .

Spanos: Sherman Paul in that, I think, very fine piece "A Letter on Rosenthal's 'Problems of Robert Creeley' " in the special issue of *boundary 2* on the oral impulse in contemporary American poetry . . .

Creeley: I thought that was a beautiful piece. I'm very grateful to him.

Spanos: . . . talks there about the first poem of *Pieces*. Let me pull it out . . .

> As real as thinking
> wonders created
> by the possibility—
>
> forms. A period
> at the end of a sentence
> which . . .

Creeley: . . . began . . .

Spanos:

> began it was
> into a present,
> a presence
>
> saying
> something
> as it goes.

You read it. I can't . . .

Creeley: Yeah, it's a kind of funny echo of Zukofsky. You know the beautiful close of that short novella, that book called "It Was"?

Spanos: No, I don't.

Creeley: It's a beautiful piece. (Reads from the piece from *Pieces*.) If I have the book, I'll show you instantly. (Goes to the bookcase.) It's a little book (returning with it) that Cid Corman published. The sentence goes on for a hundred and some odd pages. Wait a minute now. I've got the wrong damn book. This is actually two books. Wait a minute. Yeah, "It Was." No, it's a short story, excuse me . . .

It was fine weather in mid-August when I awoke anxious to go on writing the story that in the dark hours did not let me rest.

I had promised my wife not to stay up and strain my eyes, and had failed her. So I was happy to be up before she was, to tell her that I was not tired . . .

Then he goes on, you know . . .

We lived then opposite the park. . . . Thanks to the park commissioner. The park across the street, the early sun and the morning shade thrown between tall old trees, tempted me to go downstairs. . . . I wanted as I said to write, but not on paper. . . . The sentence kept me up all night. . . .

As he says, he "wants it unobtrusive to his pace." This is beautiful, I learned much from this.

I wanted as I said to write, but not on paper. I hardly ever found the park helpful to writing on paper, even in fall and winter when no one was there, especially if I were writing prose. This time it was the sentence opening the last part of a story I had worked on for months: a sentence as is often worked off paper first. The pace of narrative and interest in character do not readily help the writer's hand to set down a sentence of that order. For though characters must take things in their own stride—somewhere in his story the writer cannot hold back this sentence that judges them. . . .

To bear witness again.

He wants it unobtrusive to his pace and the characters that caused him to write. The difficulty is to judge without seeming to be there, with a finality in the words that will make them casual and part of the story itself, except perhaps to another age.

The sentence kept me up all night. . . . The halt seems likely to be permanent in the worst of the grind—when the words of an insoluble sentence written down written over, crossed out, add up to indecisions making situations and characters empty.

I feel I have not the sense in which, along with the story, I must live—and seem merely to glance at a watch.

This story was a story of our time. . . . I dusted the bookshelves. . . .

He goes on and on . . .

Still anxious to get back to my story, I became busy straightening out things about the house. Somehow we could never leave it with the necessary disarrangements of the night unsettled . . .

I'm very much like that . . .

I dusted the bookshelves and the desk of unfinished maple, and a small table of the same wood over which hung a large landscape painted by our close friend in another city: he was working on a "Defense" job—had made our walls cheerful when he had the time—and if he were coming to see us that Sunday I would gladly have put off the sentence still on my mind. I watered the plants; then covered the couch with the white cotton print handblocked in blue with early American scenes of a naval battle, Indians, date palms, mules and elephants. Why elephants happened to be drawn into scenes on authority depicting the history of St. Augustine, Florida, I have never been able to answer with the knowledge of history I have. Though I was still thinking of my story, I regretted as always that writing too often leaves little time for the pleasure of looking up answers to the unfamiliar. I found myself saying the sentence aloud.

—You were good to me.

"You were good to me." And you know, knowing him, I know that's not contrivance. It's a curious suggesting and reflecting and moving to get to where—Not to what's in mind to say that you can't say it in ways that you want to say it only. It's got to be *come to* as well as recognized as there to be said.

Spanos: Again it seems to me that the etymology of "metaphysics" is crucial here. The sentence, especially in the past tense, the "was" is a perceiving of existence from the end, that is to say, all at once, spatially. It's a recollection, a *re*-collecting in tranquillity, the tranquillity of distance, of what is essentially dispersed, *occasional*, so to speak. And this wonderful piece by Zukofsky constitutes a *beautiful* destruction or deconstruction of that objectification, that construction of the process of living in order to release it from the alienating closure of the coercive past tense. Or maybe better in order to disclose it and thus as Heidegger would say after Heraclitus to bring it near . . .

Creeley: I hear. Right . . .

Spanos: It's lovely. And of course Sherman is making the same point I think about that first poem in *Pieces* when he says:

> Creeley discards the sentence, or syntactical prescription (as, for example, in the two fragments that comprise the poem), and by transforming end, associated with the past tense, past time, and remembering in which the self is no longer in its occasion, comes into the present and the very activity of the poem. The initial, necessary and therapeutic act is to become "a presence"—one fully present and in motion, "saying / something / as it goes." In this way he avoids stasis, lives in, explores, and works through his situation.

I also like his all too brief reference to the meaning of the title *Pieces* . . .

Creeley: Pieces, yeah . . .

Spanos: . . . with all the connotations of dispersal of the breaking of the One into the many, Identity into difference. And also like the continuity suggested by this, in my mind, with your earlier work, with, for example, the title of your second book . . .

Creeley: Words . . .

Spanos: Words, not the Word but *words* . . .

Creeley: . . . but words . . .

Spanos: . . . with again all the implications of dispersal, of the dispersal at the "fall" and shatter of the comprehensive logos picture into pieces, words, the ultimate key to which is infinitely deferred.

Creeley: Yeah. You can see them flying or like senses of the *Thesaurus* or something, where one goes into two into three into four. Well, Zukofsky again was delightful to me as a younger writer. That point of his that one could spend a whole lifetime discerning philosophically the difference between the two articles "a" and "the" . . .

Spanos: Yes, you refer to this modality of dispersal in . . .

Creeley: I thought, "Right on. That's very true." You could spend a lifetime considering what order of world is in each case proposed and wherever there is a natural coming together of the two. You know, "There is a dog loose in the neighborhood." But if you say, "There is a dog loose in a neighborhood," you've got a different reality . . .

Spanos: Right . . .

Creeley: Anyhow, I don't recall that I was thinking consciously of Louis but I'm damn sure that's where those opening lines from *Pieces* came from. Because the poem goes on:

> No forms less
> than activity.
>
> All words—
> days—or
> eyes—
>
> or happening
> is an event only
> for the observer?

You see, that's my argument with the objective critics.

> ... happening
> is an event only
> for the observer?
>
> No one
> there.

There's no one there thus to observe, "Everyone / here." And
then it begins to be, you know—

> Inside
> and out
>
> impossible
> locations—
>
> reaching in
> from out-
>
> side, out
> from in-
>
> side—as
> middle
>
> one
> hand.

Yeah, that was the first determined sense. It was in that re-
spect an intention to write without overbearing decisions
about the coherence . . .

Spanos: . . . from the sentence working directly out into the
whole passage and book . . .

Creeley: Yeah. There was no book in mind as this was being
written. At one point, I think, the editor at Scribners then
wrote to ask me if I had sufficient poems in hand to constitute
another book and I read through and thought, "Yeah, I really
do." I read pretty much to the end of what I had written and
this is a tracking of time factually. But not only time. This is a
tracking of a life being lived and more or less of it is not the

point and that ending that comes to be there is there, so to speak. And I thought "That's really it."

> What do you do,
> what do you say,
> what do you think
> what do you know.

Whatever now comes will move not away, but will move elsewhere. Yeah. I guess the books, not the books but the writing to me is very useful humanly, just that it reifies senses of life lived probably more than do other realities within it. What I'm trying to say is that senses, again, of things we wanted to do, whether or not done, don't paradoxically add up to much at all. It isn't that one's dismayed by them or cynical, so as to say, "Is that all?" Things I truly wanted to do, e.g., I wanted to go see Wordsworth's house. I wanted to see the Lake District this spring. And we did. And it was terrific. I mean it was absolutely gratifying and pleasing as a place despite tourists and shifts and changes, to see his gravestone and think of Coleridge and Dorothy, for example, to see those extraordinary hills they clambered about on and equally to see where Cuthbert lived, St. Cuthbert, in Lindesfarne, the Holy Island, on the east coast. That was terrific or simply to see Basil again, sitting in a room, was as always a delight. But had I not done it, I don't think it would have—I would have probably missed doing it or only wanted to have done it, but it's what—I've just remarried and I could not humanly qualify how it was I happened ever to meet my wife, much less interest her. I don't mean to sentimentalize or to thus so quickly resolve previous relationships. But I love the people I have lived with, whether I'm now living with them or not. I'm not at all sentimental factually. I used to carry in mind a kind of aggressive sentence from Herodotus characteristically that really was dear to me. At times I would propose this to people I lived with. They'd say, "That's a rather cheap way to think of present reality." It's simply at that point when Herodotus is giving his account of the exploration to discover the source of the Nile. The particular group that's out there wandering around trying to discover this place is Egyptian and there are powers at court that don't want this exploration to take place. They're trying to discourage it. So they propose to these men that very possibly their houses and their wives and their children and their authority back in Cairo are all being wiped out while they're wandering around up here and that their very conditions as men, e.g., their families, are being thus dispersed and taken from them. And one of the more aggressive and pleasant it seems to me at least of the people simply clutches his testicles and says, "As long as we have these we have families." Well, he obviously "meant" that one way. To me what it comes to mean is that as long as one has the function, one has the life. As long as you can see, there'll be something to look at. And as long as you feel drawn to this or that human activity, you almost without your will will get it. And to discover someone who does not relate to you as some awful convenience degrading indeed to both her and yourself, you have the possibility of living. I don't really want specifically anymore than that. It's, you know—I was thinking of that situation in England. I got so bored and so irritated with the pretensions of some of my old friends even. I'm sad to relate that some of them seemed almost transformed by the meager dignity that the office had now seemingly given them. That is, they're all now at the edge of fifty or in their early fifties, so now constitute a kind of younger older generation. And seeing them so incurious about the world otherwise, seeing them sink into the kinds of containment they as young men so abhorred, seeing them tacitly being a little authoritative with the younger poets, I really felt it was offensive. I don't mean that they should wear sack cloth and propose that there is no seniority whatsoever. But I'd really prefer it. I love the way that Ginsberg constantly gives away the power he accumulates, the way he constantly puts himself in the service of the information rather than presume that it's now his authority that owns the information. Otherwise it's very grim.

Spanos: Do you see any development or movement away from certain things that you were doing early in your poetry? Is the term "development" an appropriate term for what's happened in your poems from *For Love* up to what you're doing now?

Creeley: I don't know. For example, I remember when, rather curiously, Joyce Carol Oates reviewed *Selected Poems* and in her discussion of that book she remarks that I, unlike other of my contemporaries, say, like Denise Levertov or John Ashbery, don't seem to have had a particular "development." It's as though I begin writing at some time and seem to be writing more or less that way ever since. And then there's Linda Wagner's commentary on materials of many years actually where she remarks that possibly the interest in various linguistic patterns would be the actual place of the development, you know, going from one kind of construct in language to another kind to another kind. I presume that one's—See, developing is—I always think of it in the context of "developing" one's muscles or developing photographs, as though you were *getting* somewhere. And I don't really see life as that kind of fact. I think that just as we can see the entire history of the possibilities inherent in any initial event, I presume in like sense that in human life being born is the whole, is not just the "end" of it but that which includes all that will be. Not in some fatalistic sense but I don't think there's more organically than that initial ovum that thus has been fertilized. I remember seeing on *Nova,* that television program, a few months ago an extraordinary film, using microphotography, of the spermatozoa fecundating the ovum and then the growth cycle that occurs, I think it's in the very first two or three weeks of life. *Fantastic* the way the organism multiplies. I mean, thinking of things "developing," that would obviously be where it's happening. The subsequent—again, we're thinking so didactically or the tendency is to think so didactically of two extraordinarily different tracks of development. Consciousness seems to be significant development, even as Leary put it and I think significantly. He said, "Isn't it a ridiculous fact that in our habits socially and governmentally we tend to give decisive authority to persons whose factual organic brain function is about 20 or 30 percent of its actual capacity as a usual brain? We give this extraordinary power to persons whose abilities to think in organic terms have been very much reduced." Be that as it may, the point to me is that the developing of thought would only be interesting to me insofar as it could resolve what Ginsberg says:

> yes, yes
> that's what
> I wanted,
> I always wanted,
> I always wanted,
> to return
> to the body
> where I was born.

Not to go back into the womb but actually *be* the physical event of life one obviously is.

Spanos: Heidegger calls that a repetition, the paradoxical notion of "development" which advances by returning to primordial origins. *Wiederholung,* a circularity which is not vicious, i.e., recollective. Pound calls it "making it new" . . .

Creeley: Yeah. I can see . . .

Spanos: It's a rejection of a linear notion of development. And again coming back to our reference to the hermeneutic circle much earlier, we know from the beginning but only pre-ontologically, so to speak. We know but do not know unless we become deeply and totally involved or engaged, interested, unless, as Heidegger puts it, we "leap into the circle wholly and primordially." We *repeat*, or what is the same thing, we *retrieve* constantly and that activity of repetition or retrieval generates greater and greater not knowledge but awareness, phenomenological awareness of being of what we "know" from the very beginning because we are we are be*ings*. This kind of circular understanding isn't finally a spatial understanding as, for example, the New Critical version of circular, mythic, recollective thinking is because phenomenological circularity is *interested*, not disinterested. It's in search finally of a temporal, of an incarnate not an eternal and abstract and distanced knowledge.

Creeley: See, I live in the world and I have happily friends I've known for years. But I don't have a very stable geographic location. I mean, I live here part of the year. There are friends and neighbors as the lady we met coming in, in the grocery store below, who've known me really quite intimately from my living here and know me only from my living here. It isn't that I'm hiding another life from them. But the point is my life doesn't change particularly in going to New Mexico nor did it change particularly in going to Spain last spring. I don't resist having an historical identity as a person living in a place for a significant length of time. But I don't have one. So that when I meet people thus old friends they reassert a history of me. The most dramatic and interesting occasion of it was when I'd left New Hampshire. I first lived there as a young man with my wife then and family. We'd been there about three years and become literally intimate with these people and circumstances of the place, had this old farm we were trying to bring back into productive shape, etc. Then we left that, we went away first to France where we lived for two years and another child was born, then we went to Spain and then I was momently to go to Black Mountain. I had now returned to New Hampshire to pick up an old truck and odds and ends I'd left with friends there and I went into this garage that I'd gone into many times when we lived there. I hadn't been there for three years or four years maybe. My life had been you know cataclysmic great awful all the dimensions of human experience. I walk into this garage and see absolutely as expected the habitués of the garage. They were all there. And one of them looks up looks at me and says, "Ah, Bob! I haven't seen you around lately." That was all. There was no invitation to tell them what had happened. I was instantly back in their pattern. I might have said, "But—But I was living in Spain!" But they'd say, "We don't know anything about those places." It was curiously affectionate. I mean I could have probably borrowed money or told them of some immediate need I had of that place. But to try to rehearse for them where I'd been otherwise, forget it. So I became the person that they remembered. And they didn't even remember that I wasn't there yesterday or was it three years ago? Forget it. We're here. Or seeing neighbors come back into this environment, an older man one day appeared in the street and a friend was up here with me. We'd just gone out to go somewhere and we'd met this man and he said, "Could you possibly tell me where such and such a man lives?" And gave his name. We didn't know the man. So he said he'd been away for fourteen or fifteen years, had grown up in this neighborhood and he was now returning. His wife had died and he'd been living in San Diego and he was coming back. Rather modest old suit coat, sneakers and stuff, with a little white bag with his possessions. So I took into the store. I said, "I'm sure they'll know." In an *instant* he was completely located. They knew exactly where the guy he was looking for lived and who he was himself. What I'm saying only is that there are lives one lives in relation to the accumulation of the historical patterns thus stabilized or recognized, the *histories* that permit people to have locations other than the moment to moment existence. All the relationships, all the *things* we use humanly to identify ourselves as being significantly here. At the same time there's all the factual event of *being here*, which may or may not coincide. I know that with older people as I begin myself to get older. I remember a lovely younger poet said to me once with absolutely bitter but incredible accuracy, he said, "I'm getting older but you're getting old." I thought, "Right on!" because that's what he meant, "I dig it!" And if one used language that precisely, he'd probably be interesting, no matter what his emotional context. In any case, I'm not interested in developing in the sense of getting somewhere. I *do* hear always and insistently Pound's point that after fifty, as he then was saying you can't keep your eyes on all the sprouting corn. That is, this was apropos of people asking him for help or judgment as to their activity. He said, "If you're going to get on with your own work, you've really got to do it." And therefore in some trepidation I began to think "What the hell *is* my work? I'm a poet but what do I *do* insofar as I'm a poet?" And I thought, things I would like to do would be to enact, as Olson might say, or make actual, if only for my own experience of it, the patterns and senses of person in relationships, work that for various reasons I have had to yield because I was so preoccupied by the daily shift of relationships with the family and children and myself in that maelstrom often happy at times but also at times very painful. So I'd like to—I suppose I'd like to be both more aggressive in getting to work with this preoccupation, you might say, but also to be more active in reflection.

Spanos: I detected in a number of poems that you sent me from Spain a very real sense of, a very real awareness of, growing old, of growing old and a kind of—It's almost a Yeatsian awareness of what Heidegger might call the breaking of the Instrument, which generates *real* perception. When the instrument breaks down, when, to use Heidegger's metaphor in *Being and Time,* when the hammer as a piece of equipment breaks, then you know . . .

Creeley: . . . that you're holding a real hammer . . .

Spanos: . . . then you begin to really see what the hammer is all about. What you took for granted, what thus lay hidden in habit suddenly comes out of concealment discloses itself in all its primordiality.

Creeley: Yeah, I know that you've had it.

Spanos: . . . coming back to an earlier reference to these poems where the perception is so fresh, so simple, so elemental, so primordial, I get a very strong feeling that your awareness of death, of aging, the breaking of the body, the breaking of the instrument, has generated a new power in your voice, a quiet, rich and generous power I hear in the spaces between the stark words—

> When the light leaves
> and sky's black
> no nothing
> to look at,

day's done.
That's it.

Creeley: It's a shift. In other words, as a kid having to realize unlike other kids, I'd lost an eye, I'd physically been hurt, not hurt in the sense of aching or in pain, but I'd been changed, let's say, in some physical fact, in ways that were not the common experience. So that that, in a sense, was, as a younger man, a sense that I had been *touched* by life apart from my imagination of it, e.g., I lost this eye. But I'd survived it. I'd come to an integrity despite that, just as a person who might have lost fingers realized that, yes, he could make articulate a life despite that physical loss of a leg or some part of his body that would be a usual fact in other people, deaf or blind, that he had survived. Well, that survival is so heady for awhile, even in some meager instance as the loss of one eye, which is not that functional a problem. It's not a problem but a function, rather, that gave me the sense of not being apart from physical change because, again, the eye gave me the information that, yes, of course, we change. But the place of that change was paradoxically very hard to get to. And I would characteristically give it no thought. I mean, I would stay up all night if that was the impulse or drink all night if that was the impulse. And I recognized too that you can't take care of a force that ain't there. You can't drive more slowly to save gas you don't have in the car. You know, I mean, it's a physical limit. It's like Olson's "limits are what any of us are inside of"....

Spanos: Right. Yes, and those limits or awareness of them generate authentic possibilities projective consciousness ...

Creeley: So that what I'm fascinated by is not some patient recognition let's say not some recognition that will be necessarily patient. But I'm fascinated to know how can you live an old life. You obviously could live a young one. You could live a middle-aged one. How could you live an old one? And therefore I'm very interested in not how do you do it like a how-to kit, but reading, for example, Theodora Kroeber apropos the fact that she's married to a man, I think, 40 years younger than herself. And is this a kind of grotesque idealization of herself? I really didn't think so. I think she's saying that humans live in diverse patterns. And insofar as there is mutual bond in that situation other imaginations of it may or may not be the case. I know that when Penelope and I married, when we first lived together— She's 24 years younger than myself and I thought, "God, that's what my friends always in some ways told me," not apropos of myself, but their dismay when a man or a woman married someone who seemed so disparate in relation to themselves. And I wondered therefore, was I doing simply that? Was I simply trying to be younger by marrying someone younger? And I recognized paradoxically that the marriage let me be older, let me be not "older" but let me be old as I am in age, let me be my age rather than being in a situation where I felt I was growing old and someone was using me as a measure of their getting old. That is, "if you're getting old, so must I be getting old." That's a hard trip. I don't think I'm avoiding that. But one thing, if age is not abhorrent to someone younger, it certainly is not otherwise interesting.

Spanos: Of course. Well, that poem "After," one of the two you sent me along with a letter from Spain in the spring, expresses this whole thing very, very beautifully and movingly, this letting be vis à vis the inexorable dynamics of time, which Heidegger would say is a letting *being* be:

> I'll not write again
> things a young man
> thinks, not the words
> of that feeling.
>
> There is no world
> except felt, no
> one there but
> must be here also.
>
> If that time was
> echoing, a vindication
> apparent, if flesh
> and bone coincided—

let the body be.
See faces float
over the horizon let
the day end.

Creeley: And also I find in getting older something that I'd always been rather chary about. That is, I'd insist upon trusting things, but the factual ability to trust things in me was very limited. I tended, in Pound's phrase, to "overprepare the event." I wanted to cover all possible bets. I wasn't hesitant, let's say, in taking chances apropos my own provision, you know, whether money or—But, I mean, I would take, for example, my whole family to Guatemala, not having a clue, truly, as to what we might find there, which was kind of stupid. But it wasn't that I was fearful of getting into something I couldn't get out of because I so frequently did. It was not altogether happy but it was taking care of something. But it was trying to think of all it might have as a demand too abstractly. That got to be exhausting and frustrating because (a) I could never accomplish it and (b) it was such a distraction from the real thing that was happening that I couldn't even recognize it *was* happening. I'd be waiting to see whether this or that plan was enclosing it or dealing with it. My wife Bobbie used to say that we'd go through customs, a very simple instance, and I'd be so trying to prepare to deal with customs that when they didn't ask me what was in the bag, I'd say, "Don't you want to know what's in this bag?" Because I'd so rehearsed what they would probably want to know, which was hardly protecting myself. We sure had to open a lot of bags.

Spanos: Again, what's involved, I think, is that *Care.* But I've used this other word of Heidegger's in a couple of letters to you: *Gelassenheit,* letting be or letting being be. It's a kind of recognition that to be human is to be *generous* in the face of things. The rich etymology of this word too is apropos to our subject . . .

Creeley: I remember Duncan in that beautiful poem of his where he says, "Take care by the throat and throttle it." Or I remember Ramon Sender years ago saying to me, "All you young men so care for your cares." In effect, he was saying, "It's as though it's the only proposal of your significance or seriousness that you think is possible. Your poems reek of despair and burdens." Or, say, songs like "He's Not Heavy He's My Brother," that kind of sixties sense of caring. I'd love to think that care could care. Etymologically, is it "sorrow," does it have that sense of burden? I don't know. I was talking to a friend who wrote a bright, a usefully relaxed and human discussion of Bill Merwin's poems and she speaks, as one would characteristically about his poems, of the move from childhood's integrity to the dispersal experienced then in the world and all the ways he tracks it and states it. And, of course, one would love to stay in that integrity of the child, no matter whether one liked the persons there or not. There would be that integrity nonetheless. If you hated your father, you could hate him every day. There he was. And then you get out in the street and people are more various, and may not care whether you hate them or not. They walk on by. So that movement to not the larger but that *other* world that doesn't yield to linear patterns, that just keeps happening whether you miss the boat or not, the boat that *is gone* just like the "world does not wait for flowers," as Olson puts it. I've really found that world more and more interesting. I'm bored, for example, as in Spain, when I hit old time, sad, corrupted patterns of people. They are really bleak to see. You know, people forking over their money for sleazy kinds of clothing that have a "Parisian" style or buying junk food because it was in an American cornflakes package. And I hated their suspicion and their tightness in this little corrupted town. But back in the hills a bit, in no sentimental sense, the whole ease and generosity of people seemed to return. They said hello, for example, there wasn't some awful sense of, "Here's a stranger, what can I get out of him? When is he going to bite me?" Much more open to the world. As with Basil. I *love* Basil for when we'd go about in Northern England, we'd go into a pub or something, I'd think, "*He is at home in the world.*" He sits down in a chair, it isn't that he wants to bring everybody into his conversation or wants to dominate the room. He's utterly at home. And if he has a question, he can ask it without confusion, and he can hear what's said to him without confusion. It was terrific. I thought if at 77 I have that—Yeah, if I feel as at home in the world as he does, despite the fact as he has, I've just lost my home . . .

Spanos: Yeah. That, of course, is the situation of any sensitive man in the world and I think one of the central contexts of the modern or contemporary poet. How do you achieve an at-home-ness in the context of being—Not-at-home, which is, you know, basic to the human experience. Heidegger's term is *Unheimlichkeit*, being in the realm of the uncanny . . .

Creeley: Yeah.

Spanos: . . . or, etymologically, the *notathome* which, of course, is the realm of occasion. How does one achieve at-homeness in this world in which the center, presence, as Derrida puts it, is absent? Well, again, you know, these latest poems, the poem you sent me convey . . .

Creeley: I hope they do . . .

Spanos: . . . a sense of some sort of quest for this in a way that's lost certainties, a much more lyrical, a much more, I'm almost tempted to say sentimental, but I use it in the best sense of the word, a much more *lyrical* tonality about these poems than the earlier things. There is the edge. But the edge is softer. And although it cuts, it's characterized by an uncertainty . . .

Creeley: . . . that's comfortable . . .

Spanos: . . . Well, I didn't want to say comfortable. It's not that . . .

Creeley: Well, I mean it isn't more patient, but it's more, I think, it's that letting be, in that poem I sent you. That's a good poem for me. It's like like something as simple as "let it happen," that kind of almost joking sense of "let the good times roll" or let what's going to be *be*, and don't be patient or passive or stoical. I find stoicism a bore, just that it would value nothing but its own patience . . .

Spanos: You will probably resist what I'm going to say but I still think it's there. You say, "Let what's going to be *be*." But there's something in that emphasis on *be* which opens up into a much deeper, a much profounder sense of being than simply letting it happen. I'm not sure you'd want to subscribe to this. But by letting it *be*, as I suggested earlier, you're letting *being* be. In other words, the subject matter of a lot of these poems pertains to *being*, to being in the Heideggerian sense, that is, in the ontological sense, although you know this is not a philosophical poetry. Nevertheless, if you *hear* this language rather than *see* it, as critics too often do when they read your poetry, maybe I'm imposing on it my own interest in Heidegger but I really think when I hear it. I hear something new, I don't mean in the sense of development, a deeper understanding of something that goes back to when you first used that word "occasion": "the poem is the measure of its occasion." You've *always* in your poetry, Bob, had fundamentally the deeper and profounder sense of the question, "What does being mean? What does it mean to be?" And this is not simply a matter of content, of subject matter. It is in the rhythms of your line. *It's in your voice* . . .

Creeley: I hear . . .

Spanos: . . . You're articulating, you're attempting, you're exploring, you're disclosing being. And I think you come closest to bringing it near. I mean, making it explicit without naming it in these poems. In so many of them it seems to me this is what's really happening. And I'll also say this. I think it is because you have become conscious in a way that you have never been before of the breaking of the instrument . . .

Creeley: I hear . . .

Spanos: . . . of the body going. I got this sense also when you read at Binghamton last December, even in your casual comments. So much of what you read and talked about was almost unconsciously released by your awareness of growing old.

Creeley: Yeah, I hear. I think it impossible not to be, not preoccupied but certainly thoughtful. One evening once in visiting Olson, it must have been in the sixties, we'd been up all night talking. We then walked down to the diner along the harbor there that he really enjoyed, where oftentimes the people going out to fish would come in to get some coffee and the old timers would tend to be there also, sort of watching the fishermen get it together themselves. It was a very simple diner. And we were sitting there, talking about this and that, and I suddenly realized that he was in a very intensive state of feeling and that there were tears literally coming down his face. And I reached over and said, "What's the matter, Charles?" And he said, "It's just impossible for me to," not to recognize or acknowledge, because that was tacitly what he was doing, but he said, "That the mountain can diminish and that the sea can dry up? I can't, I cannot think it. I'm balked and broken by that, that this force is tacitly diminishing. It's just horrifying to me. Threatening, very deeply threatening." Then, moments later, he was gone to England or Germany for that lecture for the Literarisches Colloquium, that would date it pretty much, 1966, I think. And then I saw him happily after that time. It didn't recur. But *that* was the fear of aging and dying, not so much the fear of death, but the fear of aging, when the power diminishes. In his context, that was really—This was what he had been *given* as a *power*, this almost problem of person with this immense size and physical strength . . .

Spanos: Yes, of course . . .

Creeley: . . . and to feel it diminishing and shifting and changing in his body was just displacing beyond all else. When he was actually dying, which was certainly not simple just that the cancer was such a tricky thing to locate as to where its source was, that was a transforming experience. But, paradoxically, in that actual situation of dying, rather characteristically he was so absorbed by the activity that he didn't really seemingly have much either fear or even, in factual sense, dismay. I speak quickly. I spent parts of, say, two or three hours two afternoons with him. Someone as Harvey Brown would have a more articulate sense of all that may have happened. But he was delighted to say, for instance, "You know, the fundament is just as rooted as the firmament." He said, ". . . my God, in times of thinking . . . ." His point was that, in times of thinking, you can actually be almost drawn to believe that the firmament is where it all goes. But, by God, the ass is the fundament, is just as much eternal.

Spanos: Tremendous. Jesus, that's tremendous.

Creeley: Yeah, it takes care of itself.

Spanos: That puts a hell of a lot more meaning into that line from "Sunday Morning," which Wallace Stevens himself learned later on the real meaning of: "Death is the mother of beauty." That's a much richer and more significant way of putting our mortality, our earthliness, than Stevens' in that early poem . . .

Creeley: Yeah, I hear . . .

Spanos: Bob, I think we've come back or come around, so to speak, to the original issue, which is worth restating, repeating, is really a better way of putting it for the light that our conversation may have shed on it. I mean, the American tradition and your relationship as poet to it. Clearly, the received, the academic version of the tradition, the one handed down to us by the New Critics, is more or less alien to your sense of it. I've already said that the New Criticism, as I see it, gives privileged status to Form or Being with a capital letter over temporality or process, being with a small letter. In other words, it prefers in a kind of basic way a poetry in which closure is ontologically prior to openness or disclosure. In doing that it seems to me it opts for a tradition in which America is subsumed under Europe. And in this understanding of the tradition it is, of course, Donne and Herbert and Crashaw and Marvell, and in America Edward Taylor, etc., at least as they're understood by the New Critics, rather than, say, Whitman, who constitute its source. What I'm saying is that the received tradition locates its ground in the Metaphysical poets, the poets who perceive *meta ta physika* and, to deconstruct one of Cleanth Brooks's favorite terms, are in*clusive* in their impulse. From this privileged point of view poets like Whitman, poets who perceive phenomenologically and are thus disclosive poets, are marginal, eccentric, so to speak. So the real poets, the poets who extend the tradition, are poets like Eliot and Auden and Frost and Tate and Ransom, centered poets who begin the poem from an end, from received assumptions about the experience it encounters and thus shapes. So that poets like Williams and Pound, the Pound of the *Cantos* and Olson and even the later Stevens and, I think, Robert Creeley, poets who return to the things themselves, who like Williams "invent" insistently, explore in the dispersed world, the divided, the occasional world in search of a new or rather a renewed measure, are outside the tradition, outside the inclusive circle, outside its bounding line its boundary. But, of course, that's where you have to be and insist on being. Let me read that great passage from Book II of *Paterson*:

> Without invention nothing is well spaced,
> unless the mind change, unless
> the stars are new measured, according
> to their relative positions, the
> line will not change, the necessity
> will not matriculate: unless there is
> a new mind there cannot be a new
> line, the old will go on
> repeating itself with recurring
> deadliness: without invention
> nothing lies under the witch hazel
> bush, the alder does not grow from among
> the hummocks margining the all
> but spent channel of the old swale,
> the small foot-prints

of the mice under the overhanging
tufts of the bunch-grass will not
appear: without invention the line
will never again take on its ancient
divisions when the word, a supple word
lived in it, crumbled now to chalk.

Anyway, that's something like the way I'd differentiate the received idea of the American tradition from your understanding of it. How would you?

Creeley: What seems to characterize it most intensively as a distinct art is its experimental nature by which I mean the fact that it's an intensive, predominantly Romantic art. I was thinking of Donald Sutherland's ways of qualifying Romanticism and Classicism. It seems to be insistently preoccupied with becoming and with time and with change, those various conditions, as opposed to space or Being or, I think . . .

Spanos: . . . stasis . . .

Creeley: . . . stasis. It's almost the dilemma that Americans, for example, when stories used to be printed in, I guess it was, *Liberty Magazine* or *Collier's* with the reading times attached, which gave, curiously, a much more intensive sense of substance, say, than if you said there was so much physical space of pages. But, more to the point, a remark of Gary Snyder's that it's space which was first used as a measure or mark of "frontier." It's thought of as something initiating and is used as a measure of persons as well, the classic frontiersman. But when there's no "space" left, we then turn speed into that possibility or resource. You accelerate and so change the experience, etc. We turn space into time into speed. But I suppose what I feel most insistently in the art is the move out from the particularities of, say, being a human person in some primary sense to the imagination of the *all else* as having the primary significance. I mean, it's as though not only in poetry and its preoccupations but equally in all terms of American life that I'm aware of, there's a constant emphasis upon *getting some-*

where. The "future," for example, is the crucial term as against terms of past or present, the future is the absolute point or center. It's ourselves becoming *there*.

Spanos: I would call this last emphasis egocentric, thus relating Olson and Heidegger again. I would also call this version of futural expectations a teleological understanding of time.

Creeley: And I can well understand how the abstraction of body was so simply accomplished. That is, the body became paradoxically a material also. As though "the mind, that worker on what is" has other aspects of information, I think, than possibly those Charles intended. The mind begins to be some kind of smelting plant for the conversion of material which ain't so happy. I know that Olson thought of it as "working" on something to gain its virtue or its actual, or to recognize its actual, nature. But it's awfully close as an image to the sense of something chomping everything up and turning it into a material of a very different order. But I, yeah, the people who are extraordinarily interesting to me are really the inventors, not the inventors in Pound's sense necessarily but the people for whom it is some insistent initiating experience. I love it. If you read it in Vaughan like, "I saw eternity the other night . . . ," I tend to hear in that as an American some incredible opening sense of physical, visionary reality. The writers anyhow that I—They aren't really crucial to me until you get to Whitman whom I came to rather late. I'm fascinated by Emily Dickinson, the interior spaces of her poems are fascinating to me. And the *factual* power of the language to state feelings is just, I think, *great*. I didn't come to Wordsworth until, really, in middle age and then recognized a very parallel power in making articulate feelings that are extraordinarily human, not that "I'm sorry for this person," but senses of how, physically, one's in the world. Extraordinary. I think that the American habit is to think of life as a testing of capacity, a measuring against something, almost a pitting of oneself against the phenomenality of all else, so that, paradoxically, not paradoxically but expectedly, there are moments of extraordinary exhaustion and blow out which sometimes are transcended magnificently like Williams in *Paterson*. I would agree with Olson again that *Paterson V* is the interesting book in that cycle, that the enclosure attempted in the first four books is really a distraction. It keeps distorting the pattern of the poem, for my reading at least. It keeps taking you into decisions rather than into—Or there are two very distinct kinds of writing going on, one wanting to make the form as a decision, the other wanting to discover the form as a function of possibility of something that *can happen* actually as opposed to something that should happen. And I find the poem to my mind of most interest in that whole time is really "The Desert Music," which I think is terrific. It's a great poem—

> Now the music volleys through as in
> a lonely moment I hear it. Now it is all
> about me. The dance! The verb detaches itself
> seeking to become articulate.

I wonder if the American habit of being *young* is a necessary factor of person and of being innocent, you know, in some curious sense of pristine condition and therefore possibility. That to me is a very deep part of our culture . . .

Spanos: How does that reconcile with the notion of occasion in the sense of being fallen? I know . . .

Creeley: Well, you see, again I characteristically thought of that sunrise. No irony. I just—"It came to pass" is the sense I feel in the word "occasion." "It was this way." "What was the occasion for your doing that?" "Well, let's see." "What were the . . ." It's not only the circumstances, what was around, the context, let's say. What was in hand, what was seemingly the case. In other respects, what was . . . "Then as I remember there were two cars here and somebody was standing there." But the occasion is what factually, as you say, *falls,* what comes to pass. And that's to me the only substantial authority in the whole event is what happened. So I love that sense I used to fear, writing occasional poems, until I probably got much more relaxed about what after all an occasion might be. I thought "I don't want to write poems celebrating the present or even particular love for persons as some didactic sense of necessity, something I have to do."

Spanos: It's true that . . .

Creeley: By the way, I don't . . . just to continue a bit on that . . . I don't really like the Adamic man theory you know . . .

Spanos: Well, this was what I was getting at when I . . .

Creeley: . . . I don't feel comfortable with that at all. It seems to me, yeah, it really seems to me reading a lot into the record that ain't there. It's like a "faux naïf" premise to me as though the European was reborn in the New World. I heard in contrast the simple statistics like Columbus' proposal to import the Indians of this country into the Old World as slaves. I just don't believe it . . . it was some other way. I mean, you get splashes in Boone or in, say, Freneau's writing or Crevecoeur's, little tastes in Bartram, who, I think, is the great writer of that extraordinary freshness at times. But I don't think there was any Adamic trip going on of any real dimension. I think it was far more the habits of Europe trying to extend to acclimatize this country to its own interests and purposes. There just never has been anything else. I think much more interesting is Olson's point that "we are the last first people."

Spanos: Yes I agree . . .

Creeley: Now that's rather different. We're the last group of human beings to arrive in a new place. So therefore our informing of it or our making a form of it has had potential. But, as Williams laments in "Asphodel," how soon we lost that "flowery bloom," how soon it was factually lost—

It was a flower
upon which April
had descended from the skies!

                              How bitter
              a disappointment!
                      In all,
                                  this led mainly
              to the deaths I have suffered.
                      For there had been kindled
                                  more minds
              than that of the discoverers
                      and set dancing
                                  to a measure,
       a new measure!
                      Soon lost.

I think there's a kind of relating to Europeans or equally a
relation to, say, Asians such as I've briefly known them. There
can be an incredibly ageless wisdom, let's say, seemingly in the
social habits of the Chinese, even some Japanese, but there's
an old *youngness* in Americans that I think is very distinct.

Spanos: Would you put Olson's point this way, or could I put it
this way? That the Europeans are fundamentally metaphysi-
cal whereas the Americans, American poets, are attempting
by the very nature of their experience to repeat to return to
origins without at the same time denying the metaphysical
thing.

Creeley: I think they include it but I think they feel . . .

Spanos: . . ."Form is never more than an extension of con-
tent." The European conceives of form as ontologically prior
to "content." The American, Whitman, say, or Williams or
Olson or Creeley, does not deny form. But "content" is onto-
logically prior to form. So that the American imagination con-
tains both the old and the new simultaneously, which is what
Olson seems to be saying there.

Creeley: Yeah, it's also in both its happy but equally in its de-
structive aspects completely unembarrassed by its appetites. It
doesn't have a form that encloses the content of the previous,
that is, in many, many ways our social habits and our ways of

seeing people have such a general schema, as witness our use of language in poetry. Our diction, so to speak, comes from such a welter of habits of professional, intellectual and social uses, none of which seem to prove a confusion. We simply use what we want to use and don't really think more about it than that. Whereas in the European pattern you can have such anomalies as Günter Grass, committed entirely to the socialist cause, particularly the working class, literally writing in a German that none of them can understand. Or the distinctions, of course, between demotic Greek and literary Greek, which again prohibits, let's say, writers of real social commitment from being understood by the people to whom their work is addressed. This happens in England too. I mean, Orwell's or, I was going to say, Shelley's moving attempts to write for the working class, to make tracts, hoping they would go along with Tom Paine's, etc. It's characteristic that it's Tom Paine who they're reading. It isn't because he speaks more plainly but because the habit of his address is more abrupt, immediate and common.

Spanos: Yeah, that's interesting, though I should point out, by the way that the revolution of the word has been taking place in Greece for a generation now. Palamas, Seferis, and above all Yannis Ritsos . . .

Creeley: I think America has—I was watching this television show apropos the Santa Fe Opera. We spend part of the year in New Mexico frequently and know some of the circumstances of the Opera and some, not happily, of the people involved. It's a rather respectable social enclave of wealthy and/or retired persons with a kind of "leisureland" feeling to it. And the Opera is their child or their pleasure. It's a very good facility. But what's interesting is, in this TV show about it, they were speaking of trying to bring the Indian children in to see the opera. They did and they seemed to like it O.K. and stuff like that. But that kind of differentiation feels very faint in this country. What I'm trying to say is that I would not go, although I might well be biased too—I would not go to those people in Sante Fe for any information concerning opera or, more particularly, art, of the situation of art, because I heard one saying, the director, John Crosby saying, you know, that Santa Fe and New Mexico was a very hospitable climate for the arts, that the arts were highly regarded. And I can think of no place that's more hostilely rejecting of its artists in actual fact. When they were there working, I don't remember anybody leaping to give Diebenkorn any extraordinary reception, and Norman Macleod was permitted to become an alcoholic— Or Ed Dorn worked for a meager pittance in the library. It isn't that they weren't recognized but even when, say, someone of actual repute to their mind as Berio, when they said, "You know this person is kind of interesting," there was still no game. What I'm trying to say there is only a social habit towards the arts, a very faint articulateness. They really wanted a party, they didn't particularly want more than that. They wanted a party that they could dominate. But what I'm trying to say is that, in this country, the fact that we do have a common imagination of democracy, whether or not we have the practical instance, means that we, that I know I as a poet feel I can speak and/or write in the nature of my own social habits and discover an audience or a company for that speech. And I would probably feel that that is a distinct American tradition, not so much the belief in people, as the experience of people in a very diverse and, you know, unstructured and . . .

Spanos: . . . *dispersed* . . .

Creeley: . . . dispersed . . .

Spanos: . . . society.

Creeley: The dilemma, of course, is we don't really know how, very significantly, to *be* anywhere. It isn't that our cities grow without structure or order, as opposed, let's say, to Paris, but that in the contemporary moment it's hard to imagine how otherwise a city would grow if it is to grow at all. E.g., if you go to Hong Kong or, particularly, to Singapore and see what's now being done with the old Chinese quarter, which is the incremental European, let's say, equivalent, forget it. It's just like highrises and condominiums. It's very American. Well, they'll say, "You did it to us." Well, to hell we did it to you. You didn't *have* to eat what was there to be eaten, if you had other choices, which you pretty obviously did. I think our naive dependence upon equality, we say an equality of education not meaning equal possibility of instruction, again I want to say, we want to say, everybody shall be able to go to Harvard. We ignore the fact as to how appropriate that would be for everybody. So we pay dues on that. We presume that all people have the right to speak equally, forgetting that some may be, you know, incapable of saying anything that's of interest in this or that specific context. But we say, "Let them speak, let them speak." We therefore have a great confusion in the arts, let's say, which is part of the tradition insofar as . . .

Spanos: Is that good?

Creeley: It's *good* because you can't nail it down.

Spanos: O.K. I like that so un-New Critical equation of confusion and tradition. That's deconstructing in a way that opens up rich possibilities. It's also letting be . . .

Creeley: Like one time in a conversation with Allen Ginsberg, I was going to go to give a lecture on Edgar Allan Poe at the Sorbonne no less, and I'd let it go up till the last minute, and I thought I'd ask my various colleagues and friends what *they* would think particularly significant about Poe. And I remember asking Allen among others, and he said, "Well, what's lovely about Poe is he's so decisively an instance of, after all, the great tradition of the poet in this country. The poet in this country is almost without exception a manifest eccentric if not a literal nut." The behavior patterns and the conduct of the poet as person in this country is a very eccentric phenomenon of being, e.g., Ezra Pound or Whitman or, again, Poe or Edwin Arlington Robinson, almost all of those one thinks of with instant and immediate affection are these very kind of cranky eccentric persons. Emily Dickinson—Again I think my resentment of Frost is that he *worked* to be that. He was a phony . . .

Spanos: That's good. He wasn't an original, an *eccentric* . . .

Creeley: I would say if I were asked to respect either man in virtue of how they seem to be persons in the world, I think that Colonel Sanders is *far* more authentic as human being, and I think his information is possibly better. Or certainly I think Colonel Sanders' fried chickens are more real than are many of Robert Frost's poems. I mean, Robert Frost makes the poem as the present Colonel Sanders' franchise makes chickens. They make them because they know they're supposed to look a certain way and have a certain use of things in order to feel like the real old timers would. And Frost won't really rock the boat if he feels it's really going to bother you. I was reading at one point in this class—I thought of a poet who again is, in this tradition, an extraordinary manifest eccentric: Robinson Jeffers. If you take Jeffers' poems and suddenly think of them in a context with Frost's, take Frost's proposed nature poems, for example, and suddenly put Robinson Jeffers' against them, he just blows them away.

Spanos: Sure.

Creeley: It isn't that he's a better poet. It's just that he *is* a poet. Frost is a versifier . . .

Spanos: . . . which means, of course, as you've been implying, he writes from the end rather than from the beginning, or, better perhaps, disinterestedly, carelessly, so to speak, rather than interestedly, *inter esse*, from in the midst of things.

Creeley: You know they're making his goddamned house in Franconia, New Hampshire, a kind of national shrine . . .

Spanos: Yeah, I've heard about that. I'm from New Hampshire and keep in touch.

Creeley: Well, then you know. Can you think of the people in that state—they've had everything else there, like ski lodges . . .

Spanos: Oh Jesus, I know . . . My . . .

Creeley: . . . and now they're going to have more. I don't know how you feel about Frost's poems but I think they take things I love and do little trips on them.

Spanos: I've always felt the same way, maybe not so strongly, about Frost's poems ever since my undergraduate years at Wesleyan where he and Sandburg were frequent visitors, were deities, and their cracker barrel poses charmed the rich New Jersey suburbanite student body. I had something to do, by the way, though it wasn't easy, just a year and a half ago with getting him off the goddamned M.A. reading list and getting Olson—and you know how tight those reading lists are—getting Olson and Wallace Stevens, the late Wallace Stevens, on it in poetry, and Beckett and Pynchon in fiction.

Creeley: That's great . . .

Spanos: But I had—It was painful trying to get Frost off. I finally—I don't think I persuaded anybody that these were good writers or that Frost wasn't, but I did finally make the point that this postmodern writing really existed and had to be represented in any graduate list presuming to reflect the real situation of letters in America.

Creeley: One time visiting Allen in Cherry Valley, he showed me an anthology, then contemporary, that his father had given him in grammar school or something like that. And it was like just over the edge of the 19th century into the 20th. So that Robinson Jeffers was in there. It seems to me Browning was in there, and so on. It was like the poets of England and America. And Frost was there as some kind of almost late 19th century Edwardian poet. And Allen, not knowing at all then who Frost was, had pencilled a little moustache on him and written underneath, "Hitler." The only time I was ever thrown out of a class in school, and I had no perception of what I was doing otherwise, in fact, the teacher was an extraordinarily pleasant man, a very dear teacher in my estimation, it was an English class, I guess I was a junior in high school and we were now reading modern poetry. We were reading Eliot and, you know, the typical poetry we would have read. And we came upon Frost and those "two roads." "Two roads diverged in a yellow wood . . . ." And I began sort of glibly but nonetheless effectively to parody the poem, to say, "Well, I don't understand why he's saying that—Will he ever know where the other road led to? Why is he so *smug* about it?" I was really irritated by his patness. And the teacher, who was doing his job like any of us, was really impatient that I was getting the whole class laughing and nobody was paying attention to the poem. So finally he asked me to leave. And then later he said "Come around and see me tonight." And so in the process of discipline he said, "You know, I can understand what you feel about Frost but I don't agree to your wanting to impose it on all the other members of the class. Simply respect that someone might not agree with you apropos of Robert Frost and let them have their chance. What I think of Frost is really immaterial but I certainly don't think your attitude toward Frost should dominate the entire class period when we're supposedly studying his work." Frost's the only person that ever excited me like that, really made me gleefully angry and wanting to . . .

Spanos: You were deconstructing the expectations in that classroom. You're a natural deconstructor, Bob.

Creeley: Yeah, I was in those days. Well, for instance, I remember we were put to memorizing a poem which we really liked, that sense of memorizing a poem of your own interest and then you come to class and write it out. And so I did and the teacher then called me in afterwards handed the paper back. I'd got the whole first line wrongly. And he said, "How in the name of heaven could you do that?" He said, "You were writing that poem of Emily Dickinson's and her line is 'Inebriate of air am I.' That's kind of simple if you remember the rest of the poem. You've got 'I am an inebriate of air' " . . .

Spanos: Great! That's great . . .

Creeley: . . ."that thing doesn't have any rhythm or anything to it." But I couldn't say, "Inebriate of air am I." It sounded silly. I was going to straighten it out for her.

Spanos: That's tremendous. So that impulse of the voice to begin from the beginning, in other words, well, don't know if it's "in other words" . . .

Creeley: . . . back to the tradition?

Spanos: Yeah. What I wanted to say is that, in other words, I'm not sure it's in other words. "In the American grain" is, means, that there *is* no American grain.

Creeley: Well, I suppose as with Olson or Melville or any of the writers, Pound very much, reading Pound's early *Patria Mia*, the imagination there, Whitman, I suppose, has the most expansive view. I find myself both really drawn to Thoreau, let's say, but also very irritated with him. Emerson, of course, I keep being moved by the journals, but the poems really basically leave me cold. It's, I suppose, the tradition is that, trying to not humanize but trying to think of human possibility in this extraordinarily curious country. I was thinking of Penelope off to Idaho. She must drive two three four days, possibly, before she gets there. She was first here, coming from this island culture, New Zealand, although she had been to Europe, etc., etc. She flew into Buffalo, as it happens, and then we started driving to New Mexico. It was just phenomenal to her. She'd never seen a land mass like this before and people continuously speaking American. And we still had a thousand miles to go if we were going to the West coast. It's a—I find it a very diverse country. I mean by that I don't think the melting pot symbol is at all useful or in any sense adequate.

Spanos: No, the notion of the alchemical pot out of which the quintessence emerges, the *center*, the *logos*, the *word*, the word that recollects the fragmented One after the fall into time and reestablishes, transforms, the iron into the golden age that won't do, as you've said before, to describe America. *Again dispersal* . . .

Creeley: . . . dispersal . . .

Spanos: . . . *That's* the grain. It's dispersal. I like and, of course, it seems to me that Williams in *Paterson*, that's what that whole poem is about.

Creeley: Yeah . . .

Spanos: Dispersal and, of course, *descent.*

Creeley: "The descent beckons" . . .

Spanos: . . ."The descent beckons." The ascent *beckoned* past tense, the descent *beckons* present tense.

Creeley: "Memory" . . .

Spanos: So fall, dispersal, infinite deferral, of that ultimate and final *thing* . . .

> The descent beckons
>   as the ascent beckoned.
>   Memory is a kind
> of accomplishment,
>   a sort of renewal
>   even
> an initiation, since the spaces it opens are new places
>   inhabited by hordes
>   heretofore unrealized,
> of new kinds—
>   since their movements
>   are toward new objectives
> (even though formerly they were abandoned).

No defeat is made up entirely of defeat—since
the world it opens is always a place
                    formerly
unsuspected. A
world lost,
            a world unsuspected,
                        beckons to new places
and no whiteness (lost) is so white as the memory
of whiteness

Olson too must have had this in mind when he wrote that goddamned beautiful book *Call Me Ishmael*, because what is it that Ahab is going after in his obsessive, his mad pursuit of the white whale? Ahab is going after that *one final thing*, or rather *no*-thing, you see . . .

Creeley: Right, right, right . . .

Spanos: . . . in the context, of course, of a universe, of a nature of things which will not allow it, you know, because . . .

Creeley: I think, and absolutely, Bill, I hear it as the—He's *measuring* himself, the final thing that can declare his event in the world.

UNDER DISCUSSION
Donald Hall, General Editor

Volumes in the Under Discussion series collect reviews and essays about individual poets. The series is concerned with contemporary American and English poets about whom the consensus has not yet been formed and the final vote has not been taken. Titles in the series include:

Forthcoming volumes will examine the work of Langston Hughes, Muriel Rukeyser, and H.D., among others.

Please write for further information on available editions and current prices.

Ann Arbor   The University of Michigan Press

Printed and bound by CPI Group (UK) Ltd, Croydon, CR0 4YY

13/04/2025

14656507-0001